Better Homes and Gardens

Celebrate

Volume 5

contents

begin

spring

food

summer

96 CELEBRATE warm weather with fun projects that make every day special. From Father's Day to a new school year, this chapter offers gift and party ideas to boost you to the top of the thoughtfulness scale. Plus, add seasonal accents to your home, using new creative techniques.

boo

124 UNLEASH your inner fiend with outrageous projects that make Halloween magic. Whether you prepare for trick-or-treaters on the block or host a full-blown masquerade bash, here's all you need to make a monster of a success. Recipes, decorations, pumpkins—it's all at your beck and call.

easy does it

TAKE YOUR TIME—these crafts take little time and money, plus they are fun to make, show, and share.

MEREDITH CONSUMER MARKETING
Vice President, Consumer Marketing: Janet Donnelly
Consumer Marketing Product Director: Heather Sorensen
Consumer Marketing Product Manager: Wendy Merical
Consumer Marketing Billing/Renewal Manager: Tami Beachem
Business Director: Ron Clingman
Senior Production Manager: Al Rodruck

WATERBURY PUBLICATIONS, INC.
Contributing Editor: Sue Banker
Contributing Art Director: Cathy Brett
Contributing Copy Editor: Peg Smith
Contributing Proofreader: Gretchen Kauffman

Editorial Director: Lisa Kingsley
Creative Director: Ken Carlson
Associate Editors: Tricia Bergman, Mary Williams
Associate Design Director: Doug Samuelson
Production Assistant: Mindy Samuelson

BETTER HOMES AND GARDENS® MAGAZINE
Editor in Chief: Gayle Goodson Butler
Executive Editor: Oma Blaise Ford
Managing Editor: Gregory H. Kayko
Creative Director: Michael D. Belknap
Senior Deputy Editor, Food and Entertaining: Nancy Wall Hopkins

MEREDITH NATIONAL MEDIA GROUP
President: Tom Harty

MEREDITH CORPORATION
Chairman and Chief Executive Officer: Stephen M. Lacy

In Memoriam: E.T. Meredith III (1933–2003)

change is good

I've always agreed with the adage that we're all gifted in one way or another.

Maybe you're a cooking connoisseur, a crafting queen, or decorating is right up your creative alley. And just maybe you aspire to be a magician that can do it all. No question: You can!

Every now and then, when out of our element or out of ideas, we can all use an inspiring friend to help out along the way. That's where *Better Homes and Gardens Celebrate, Volume 5,* steps in.

Guests will rave over the delicious tried-and-true recipes. Friends will more than appreciate your thoughtfulness when they open handcrafted treasures that come from the heart. And you will love coming home to beautifully decorated rooms that shine with seasonal flair.

From the first day of the new calendar year right up through that bewitching day in October, *Celebrate* offers a plethora of inspiring ideas that make each day festive, each get-together memorable, and each season enchanting.

So go ahead, work a little magic. No one has to know how easy it is.

Wishing you the best of every season,

Sue Barker

LET THE YEAR
begin
A CLEAN SLATE

STARTING FRESH

Revamp your decorating style with imaginative ideas leading the way. Fun patterns, feel-good colors, and holiday surprises start off the new year artistically.

Word Nerd

Play around with kitchen décor using wood letter tiles to spell out the fun. These projects score big points using game pieces and crafts store replicas.

Service with a Smile

An unfinished wood tray scores big when lined with oversize letter tiles. Spell out food-theme words horizontally for added interest. Glue the pieces in place or leave them loose so others can take a turn at their spelling.

Organized to a T

Keep kitchen counters and cabinets tidy with letter tile labels. Low on letters or space on containers? Use a single letter to initialize contents of containers.

Charmed, I'm Sure

Let guests join in the fun with glasses labeled with initials. Drill a tiny hole in the upper left corner of each letter tile and thread with a small length of ball chain.

Double Duty

Mark guest's places at the table with a personalized clothespin to hold napkin pleats in place. Paint a clothespin to coordinate with your color scheme or check options where scrapbook supplies are sold.

All Shook Up

Tell at a glance salt from pepper by painting shakers different colors of glass paint. To frame a letter tile, mask off a square slightly larger than tile; paint black, then let dry. Dip a pencil eraser into paint; dot on surface. Paint tile edges to match each shaker. Let paint dry and follow paint manufacturer's instructions for curing. If baking is required, remove stoppers first. Use strong adhesive to bond a tile to each shaker.

Words to Live By

A pre-cut wood plaque, approximately 10×8, makes an ideal base for a kitchen reminder. Use 2-inch tiles for KISS and 1-inch tiles and a blank for the remaining phrase. Paint the plaque as desired and glue the tiles in place.

Dip Stick
Make food markers in a jiffy. Simply glue painted-edge letter tiles to toothpicks or skewers then poke in place.

Goodies to Go
Personalize gift bags with monograms. While these bags had chalkboard shapes already in place, you could add chalkboard stickers to plain bags for a similar look.

Chip Clips
Keep a tight seal on chip bags with these lighthearted clips. Choose clips large enough to hold up to five 1-inch tiles.

Great Combo
Turn serving pieces into statements with letter tiles. Keep in mind that flat surfaces are best for attaching letter tiles. Just glue in place with strong adhesive for the surfaces being joined, then let the fun begin.

Birthday Fun

Celebrate with a watercolor-theme gathering that comes alive with brushes of greatness.

To the Letter

You won't be at a loss for words! Use papier-mâché letters to exclaim enthusiasm. Use 12-inch-tall papier-mache letters to spell HOORAY. Use a crafts knife to carefully cut off the front of each letter, leaving the sides intact. Measure the depth of the letter. From three colors of crafts foam, cut several strips at differing lengths. Roll each strip tightly; hot-glue the ends. Hot-glue rolls to the front of each letter in gradational patterns. Place the rolls together tightly to fill the space.

Color All Around

Enliven plain white paper lanterns with strokes of watercolors to carry on the party theme. Use a wide foam brush to paint the top and bottom of each lantern in two coordinating colors, such as yellow and orange or blue and purple. Then mix the colors together to paint the center and blend the shades.

Sweet Treats

Brush white crepe paper streamer lengths with two shades of watercolor paint; let dry. Overlap two colors slightly and machine-stitch the lengths together. Gently gather to make a slight ruffle. Use double-sided tape to embellish candy jars with the fancy strips.

Set the Table

Place watercolor-inspired creations on a background of white to create subtle drama. Choose a white tablecover and white plates so the runner, napkins, place cards, and flower jars are in the limelight.

Clearly Different

Mason jars are versatile. Transform them into flower vases with colored-glass paint. Just brush a light coat of paint onto the exterior of the jar in one direction using a foam brush then let it dry. Apply a second light coat in the opposite direction.

Spell It Out

Letter stickers are used to create the lettering on these place cards. To help dull the adhesive, adhere and remove stickers on the back of your hand several times before placing letters on card front. Brush the card front with similar watercolor paints and combine the colors to blend for a gradational effect; let dry. Remove letter stickers from each place card.

At the Plate

Show your true colors with a pretty presentation at each place setting. Paint a large doily with splashes of watercolor for a liner on each plate. Use a strip of candy buttons as a napkin ring around a dip-dyed napkin and tableware. To make the invitation, use a small paper doily as a mask. Print "You're Invited" on the front of a blank card using a computer printer. Center a paper doily over lettering and firmly hold it in place. Paint around doily with assorted watercolor paint. Dip a cotton swab in paint to dab doily edging. Remove doily and let paint dry completely.

Sweet Somethings

Mini clay dishes and Valentine greetings make grand gestures, especially when handmade with love.

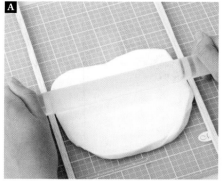

Tokens of Affection

Treat your sweetie to a little dish that's just the right size to hold love notes, jewelry, or a decadent piece or two of chocolate.

WHAT YOU'LL NEED

white oven-bake clay (such as Sculpey)
acrylic roller
wooden rods
die-cut circle or heart shape
toothpick
items for texturizing the clay: pencil eraser, rubber stamp, paper doilies
ink pad in desired colors
small round paper bowl
baking sheet
fine-grit sandpaper
foam paintbrush
acrylic paint
fine-tip artist's paintbrush (optional)
decoupage medium (such as Mod Podge)

WHAT YOU DO

1. Following manufacturer's instructions, condition the clay. Place clay on a smooth, hard surface. Using acrylic roller, roll out clay to ¼-inch thickness. To roll, position a wooden rod on each side of the clay, place the roller across the clay and wooden rods; roll the clay to a consistent thickness, as shown in Photo A.
2. For a circle or heart-shape dish, lay die-cut circle or heart shape on the flattened clay. Trace around the shape with a toothpick to cut it out, as shown in Photo B. Jagged edges will be sanded in Step 7.
3. Using texturizing items of your choice, stamp or emboss the clay with a pencil eraser or rubber stamp. Press eraser or stamp into ink pad then press the design into the clay, as shown in Photo C.
4. For lacelike embossing, place a stack of six paper doilies on the clay then roll over the doilies with the acrylic roller until an impression is made, as shown in Photo D. Carefully remove the doilies from the clay surface.
5. Place a small paper bowl right side down on a baking sheet. Place clay right side down on top of bowl, gently pressing the edges of the clay to round them against the curve of the bowl.
6. Following clay manufacturer's instructions, bake the clay. Allow clay to cool thoroughly.
7. Sand the dish with fine-grit sandpaper; wipe off sanding dust.
8. Using a foam paintbrush, paint the dish with acrylic paint, if desired. If needed, use a fine-tip paintbrush to paint in grooves, ridges, or stamped areas; remove excess paint with paper towel. Let the paint dry.
9. Paint the dish with decoupage medium; let dry.

Follow Your Heart

Set your sights on a greeting card with stitched baker's twine details. Cut out three 1-inch-wide heavyweight paper hearts. Brush decoupage medium or crafts glue onto one side of each heart then sprinkle with silver glitter; let dry. Using a sewing needle, stitch baker's twine feathers through the card as shown. Cut a bamboo skewer into three 3-inch-long pieces for arrows. Glue the skewers and hearts in place. Print out a three-word message on colored paper; cut out. Use glue stick to adhere printed words to contrasting paper then trim narrow borders. Glue message close to arrow tips, as shown above.

Sharing Shamrocks

Celebrate St. Patrick's Day with little unexpected surprises
for all your Irish friends.

Luck in Bloom

Irish or not, spread good fortune
with a shamrock plant, aka Oxalis.
These plants are widely available
and fit nicely in container gardens
come summer. Add a handwritten
tag to identify the bit o' green.

Going Green

Wrap inexpensive plain glass votive holders in green shamrock-like fabric to bring their beauty to light. Cut fabric to fit around each holder. Brush a coat of decoupage medium on the glass, wrap with fabric, then apply another coat of sealer on top; let dry. Insert candles. With cardstock name tags, tied on with waxed twine or embroidery thread, the votives can be set as place cards or party favors, or given as good-luck wishes to Irish family and friends.

Over and Under

Weave strips of felt for a neat and tidy lattice table runner that's simpler than it looks. Cut a 9-inch-wide piece of felt to the desired length and several 1½×10-inch strips for lattice. Mark lines 1½ inches apart in disappearing ink on the length of the runner. Using a crafts knife or a rotary cutter, cut strips along lines in runner, leaving a 1½-inch uncut border at both ends. Weave strips of felt into runner as shown in Photo A, creating a pattern and leaving gaps between sections as desired. Pin the ends in place and sew around the runner ½ inch from the edge. Trim excess at strip ends.

All the Right Angles

Versatile crafts felt takes a starring role in
geometric accents that add practical beauty.

A

B

Clever Catchall

Felt comes in a range of weights. Thick felt is difficult to cut, but it is generally sturdy and smooth. This stylish catchall gets structure from midweight 3-millimeter-thick felt. Use packing tape on the underside to attach the pattern from page 155 to the felt sheet, as shown in Photo A. Cut out the felt shape using sharp scissors; notch each corner, stopping at the marked point on the pattern. Pinch together the cut corners and sew together using a straight stitch and matching thread, as shown in Photo B.

Dot Matrix

Crafts felt combines with thick felt pads designed for furniture to make this pop art-inspired rug. Cut out 36 felt circles in a variety of colors, using one 3-inch-wide felt pad as a pattern. Attach circles to the adhesive side of the felt pads. Arrange the circles in a pleasing grid pattern then flip them over so the protective pads face up. Cut strips of neutral-color ½-inch-wide cotton trim for each row to match the length and width of the rug. Attach the cotton trim to the felt pads using fabric glue, as shown in Photo A; let dry for 24 to 72 hours before using.

No-Quilt Coaster

Dense wool felt—usually found on a bolt and purchased by the yard—is ideal for heavy-use items such as these sophisticated coasters. To make them, use the patterns on page 155. Trace and cut out a star and circle from neutral-color felt and paper-backed fusible web, such as Wonder-Under. Apply the fusible web to the corresponding felt shapes. Cut diamonds from a variety of felt colors, using packing tape to hold the patterns in place, as shown in Photo A. Remove fusible web paper backing from the star shape to expose adhesive, then fuse diamonds in place on the star, as shown in Photo B. Fuse a circle to the back of each coaster for added padding, as shown in Photo C.

Hello, Mardi Gras

Wherever you live, host a party with the glitz and
festivities of the New Orleans Mardi Gras.

Delightful Disguise

Welcome guests to the table with masks made especially for them. Purchase blank masks at a crafts store to decorate with braid, feathers, and acrylic gems. Craft each mask differently and be sure to take photos of guests wearing the mysterious creations.

Fancy Favor

Candy favor cups add pizzazz to a Mardi Gras party. Press adhesive-back gems to each cup, in a pattern. Glue a feather to one side. For the finishing touch, glue a length of beading around the bottom edge of the cup.

Bedazzled Charger

Give a metallic gold charger a glamor nudge. Adhere a small arrangement of gems on one side of a charger then hot-glue beads around the rim.

Bead Box

Ensure each guest has beads to wear at the party. Trim small cardboard boxes with colorful ribbon glued in place. Press on a few adhesive gems for extra wow.

Easy Does It
Be Mine

Key to My Heart

Let your sweetie know he's your one and only. Brush the lid of a heart-shape candy box with decoupage medium; sprinkle with glitter and let dry. Tie a key, available with scrapbooking and crafting supplies, with a ribbon bow then hot-glue it to the top of the candy box.

Notes of Love

Adore your Valentine by draping visible messages of love. Back 2-inch squares, cut from white cardstock, with red paper; trim a narrow border. Adhere to pink glitter paper and trim a narrow border using deckle-edge scissors. Attach the sentiments to a cord with red glittered clothespins.

Cookie Cutter Idea

Make a mini tray just big enough to hold a couple chocolate hearts. Trace a heart-shape cookie cutter on the wrong side of pink glitter paper. Trim ½ inch beyond the line using decorative-edge scissors. Center cookie cutter on the right side of the heart. Dot with hot glue on the edge of the cookie cutter to adhere it to the paper. Glue a ribbon end to side of cookie cutter, wind the ribbon around the heart, and glue remaining end in place.

Sweet Treat Jars

In minutes make a stash of adorable candy holders for those you hold near and dear. Wrap small jars with wide ribbon and hold in place with a cord bow. Fill the jars with skewered gumdrops in traditional red and white shapes.

Frilly Treat Cups

These little cuties steal hearts in a heartbeat. To trim, place double-sided tape around top. Cut 1-inch squares of tissue paper. Place a square on a pencil eraser, twist, and place ruffled tissue paper onto tape to cover.

spring

A TIME TO RENEW

ENJOY

As the season blooms gloriously, enhance your home with beautifully fresh projects.

Easter Egg Extravaganza

Make colorful, patterned Easter eggs sing with fabric, tissue paper, glitter, markers, and a variety of adhesives.

Fun Fabric

Add springtime flair to your home with delightful fabric-covered eggs. Attach fabric remnants to a double-sided adhesive sheet, smoothing out air bubbles. Cut the sheet into strips, remove the backing, then attach to eggs.

Terrific Washi Tape

Cut geometric shapes from Washi Tape to adhere to eggs. Vary lengths and sizes of shapes to create an eye-catching egg display.

Lovely Lines and Lace

Cut narrow tissue paper strips and punch doily borders for a dainty egg. Brush matte decoupage medium onto the eggshell, then carefully lay tissue pieces in place.

Glamorous Glitter Stripes

Create vibrant bands of color by attaching ⅛-inch-wide double-sided adhesive strips to eggs. Pour different colors of glitter into separate shallow bowls. Remove the backing from one strip of adhesive and, starting with the darkest color, firmly roll the egg in glitter. Remove excess glitter with a clean paintbrush. Repeat for each color.

Totally Tattooed
Bright, colorful, and simple-to-apply temporary tattoos stick to eggs quickly with no clean up. With a steady hand, use a damp sponge to press and hold images on the shell for a full 30 seconds. Remove and let dry.

Pastel Stripes
Cut a variety of pastel Washi Tape in narrow strips to decorate a bowlful of eggs. Attach strips to the egg, overlapping tape at top and bottom.

Magic Marker
Pretty modern, chic, patterns are simple to draw. Simply use colored permanent markers to draw designs. Go freestyle, where lines of any size and shape add character.

Pretty Polka Dots
Punch circles from double-sided adhesive tape with a crafts punch; attach circles to eggs. Pour different colors of glitter into separate bowls. Roll each egg in glitter; remove excess with a clean paintbrush. For multicolor eggs, place a few stickers on an egg at a time. Roll in glitter, remove excess, adhere more circles, and repeat with a different color.

Springtime Bliss

Make a big statement with tiny flower arrangements.

Coffee Break

Arrange a handful of flowers in a few cups and saucers for beautiful displays. Mismatched coffee cups stacked on saucers and a cake pedestal create a casual "skyline" floral centerpiece.

Salad Days

Investigate the vegetable drawer for makings to decorate clear cylinder vases. Pair deep green leaf lettuce with purple hyacinth, and rainbow chard stems with pink roses. Place a water-filled container inside each cylinder vase. Cut veggies about the same height as the vase and insert between containers. Arrange flowers in the inner container and finish with a quick wrap of colorful twine.

Dish Fulfillment

Instead of making a soufflé—turn that dish into a pretty basket for the table. Cut floral foam to fit dish, soak until moist, then set in the dish. Cut tulip stems so blooms peek out the top of the dish. Use an unsharpened pencil to bore holes in the foam for stems, then insert tulips tightly to create a pave effect. For a handle, loosely twist two or more branches together, securing the ends with floral wire, then insert into the dish. Finish with a colorful burst of ranunculus, daffodils, or other small blooms.

All Afloat

As you gather around the table this spring, let conversation flow over with a low-profile centerpiece full of floating flowers. For extra-special mood lighting, float glowing candles among the blooms.

Simply Easter

Catch spring fever with quick-and-easy decorating and egg-hunt ideas for an eventful gathering.

Stephen

Paper-Bunny Place Cards

These oh-so-cute place cards are perfect for a casual Easter brunch. Fold 4×6-inch pieces of pink cardstock in half lengthwise. Write each guest's name on the left side of the folded card, and use a white paint pen to draw each bunny face as shown. Cut ears from scraps of pink cardstock then use the paint pen to add details. Secure ears to the card using a dab of glue; let dry. Fold over one ear for whimsy.

Dynamic Napkin

Trace an egg shape on one corner of a cloth napkin. Use ⅛-inch tape to make intersection lines running through the egg pattern. Using soft fabric paint, brush in the egg shape; let dry 5 minutes then remove tape. Let paint dry.

Tiered Easter Egg Centerpiece

Create a bold centerpiece with graphic stripes on dyed eggs. Wrap eggs with rubber bands then dunk them in dye. Wash rubber bands well between uses to avoid transferring dye. A two-tier dish displays egg-filled nests for a pretty (and easy to make) centerpiece. Complement the bold colors of the centerpiece with single-color name cards and napkins with an Easter egg-shaped pattern.

Easter Bonnet Basket

Move the party outdoors, and improvise an Easter basket centerpiece with a straw hat filled with speckled eggs and greenery. Hollowed-out eggs can be stuffed with paper ribbons that include spring wishes or egg-hunting clues.

Fabric-Wrapped Easter Pails

Decorate tin pails and planters to stand in for egg-gathering. Apply decoupage medium to pails, then smooth on fabric cut to fit, allowing overlap and openings for handles. Apply decoupage medium over the fabric, then let dry completely.

Bring on the Derby

To celebrate the Kentucky Derby, cut out horse silhouettes to prance in flower arrangements. Top a bowl of fortune cookies with colorful fabric versions, filled with clever words of wisdom.

When in doubt, give it a good guess.

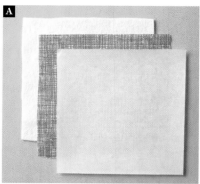

A

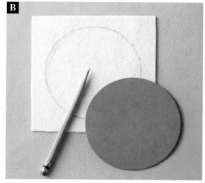

B

C

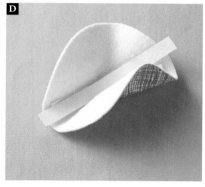

D

Derby Fortune Cookies

Turn fabric scraps into keepsake fortune cookies with personalized messages tucked inside.

WHAT YOU NEED
fabric
felt
iron-on adhesive
circle pattern, page 157
18- or 20-gauge wire
quick-setting gel glue
paper fortune strips

WHAT YOU DO
1. Cut fabric, felt, and iron-on adhesive into 4½-inch squares as shown in Photo A. Following manufacturer's directions, use iron-on adhesive to fuse fabric to felt for one layered square.
2. Print and cut out circle pattern from page 157. Trace and cut out circle on fabric square as shown in Photo B.
3. Cut wire and a strip of felt slightly shorter than diameter of circle. Glue wire to felt strip, then glue felt strip to circle, wire side down as shown in Photo C. Let dry 10–15 minutes.
4. Place fortune strip inside the circle. Fold the circle in half along the wire, then bring the ends of the wire together to shape a fortune cookie as shown in Photo D.

Pony Up

In honor of the derby, use the patterns on page 156 to cut horse silhouettes from coordinating papers for the table. Use chopsticks or skewers to hold the cutout, hiding the tip with the saddle. For the base, use a bamboo steamer lined with plastic and floral foam. Arrange flowers in steamer and push stick into foam.

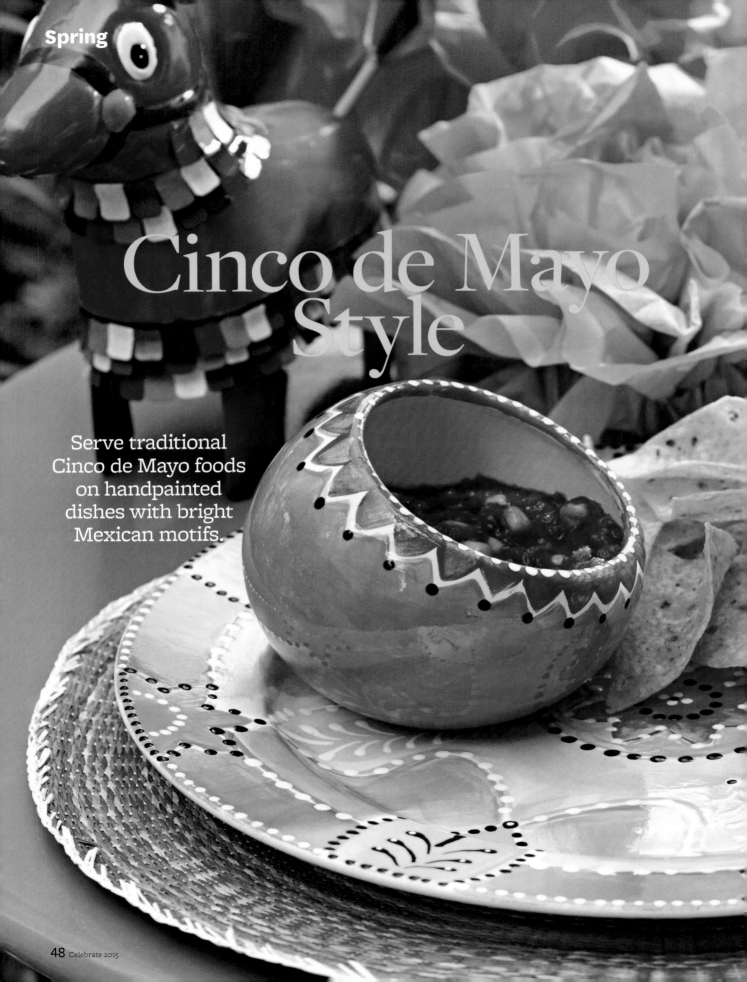

Cinco de Mayo Style

Serve traditional Cinco de Mayo foods on handpainted dishes with bright Mexican motifs.

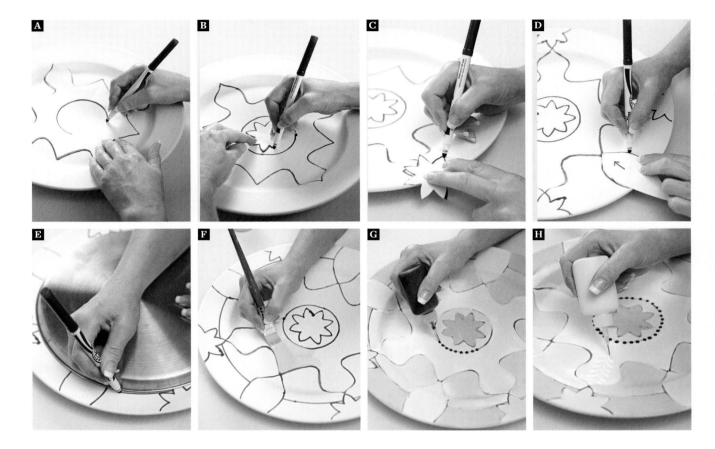

Party Pottery

Paint-your-own pottery studios are ideal places to make these bright tabletop pieces. While they look as professionally done as purchased serving pieces, these are easy enough for beginning painters to make. For help in locating a pottery studio, see Sources, page 160.

WHAT YOU NEED

sponge and water

large bisque plate or platter, dip bowl, and pair of margarita glasses

pencil and tracing paper

scissors

inexpensive marking pen in any color that disappears when pottery is fired

round object, such as a stovetop burner cover, plate, bowl, or baking pan approximately 3 inches smaller diameter than bisque plate

paints for bisqueware: light turquoise, medium turquoise, orange, yellow, lime green, red, black, and white

paintbrushes

paint dot bottles: black and white

WHAT TO DO

1. Use a water-dipped sponge to wipe all surfaces of bisque pieces.

2. Trace and cut out the patterns on page 158. Center the large medallion pattern on the plate; trace around pattern and the inner circle with a marking pen, as shown in Photo A. Place flower pattern in the center; trace as shown in Photo B.

3. Arrange and trace flower pattern on plate rim, as shown in Photo C.

4. Place the leaf pattern (arrow toward plate center) and trace partial leaf at each remaining medallion tip, as shown in Photo D.

5. Center round object on plate; trace as shown in Photo E.

6. Paint the large medallion light turquoise, as shown in Photo F; let dry. Paint a second coat and let dry. Note: Colors will darken when piece is fired.

7. Paint the center flower red, the circle around flower lime green, the round area around medallion medium turquoise, the partial flowers lime green, and leaves yellow. Let each section dry then paint a second coat; let dry.

8. Use the black paint dotter to outline the center circle, as shown in Photo G.

9. Use the white paint dotter to draw feather strokes on each long medallion section as shown in Photo H.

10. Referring to the photo, pages 48–49, dot and add feather strokes as shown using the black and white dotter bottles; let dry.

11. For margarita glasses, trace a partial leaf or partial flower onto each glass base. Paint using the same techniques as on the plate; let dry.

12. For the dip bowl, paint a red scallop around bowl rim; let dry. Paint on a second coat and let dry. Paint the remainder of the bowl using the same techniques as on the plate; let dry.

13. Fire the painted serving pieces at a pottery shop.

Fiesta Cups

Give paper cup favors an edge with festive tissue paper pieces. Cut 1-inch squares from a variety of bright tissue papers. Place a pencil eraser in the center of a tissue paper square then twist pencil. Dab the twisted end in thick crafts glue then press under rim of paper cup; gently remove pencil. Alternate colors around the rim.

Grand Glasses

No need for glass markers when you paint the base of each margarita glass a little differently. Use the same technique as used for the serving pieces, opposite.

Contained Creativity

Use a plain vase as a blank canvas to express your creativity. There are no rules when it comes to doodling—just grab your paint pens and start drawing. Or, if you're not confident of your freehand abilities, sketch a design on paper and use transfer paper to position the design on surface.

Oodles of Doodles for Mom

Make Mom smile with useful containers decorated with your very own doodles.

Tea Time

Plain white ceramic kitchen accessories are inexpensive, readily available, and perfect for embellishing with paint pens. Use the patterns on page 157 and transfer paper to imitate this look, or use your imagination to draw your own designs. To use pattern, trace onto white paper; cut around the outside of the pattern. Cut a piece of transfer paper slightly larger than the area to be doodled. Tape the pattern over the transfer paper, as shown in Photo A. Using a pencil, firmly trace the pattern lines to transfer design to surface, as shown in Photo B. Remove the pattern and the transfer paper. Using a paint pen, trace the lines as shown in Photo C; let dry. Cure the paint by baking the piece in the oven, following manufacturer's instructions.

Going Global
An instant "guest book," this globe will become a keepsake conversation piece. Arm guests with permanent marking pens to write a little ditty or a doodle.

The Journey Begins

Globes and maps lay the foundation for a super-cool graduation party theme that's big on fun and easy on decorating funds.

Navigate Your Way

Set the stage for a travel-theme graduation party with compass-style invitations. Choose a graduation photo that crops nicely into a 2-inch circle. Print the photo on heavy paper then cut out. For each invitation, from scrapbook papers, cut out two 4-inch circles from a dark color and two 3-inch circles from a light color. Cut a 2-inch circle from a subtle-pattern paper. Use a brad to attach a compass arrow (available with scrapbook supplies or clock making kits) to the center of one patterned circle. Use sticker letters to add N, S, E, and W to the compass. Use a fine marking pen to write "The Journey Begins..." around compass and party specifics around photo. Edge each paper circle with scrapbooking chalk. Using the photo as a guide, attach paper circles using glue stick. Add an eyelet to compass and photo circles as shown. Connect circles using ball chain. Line each envelope with map paper or an outdated atlas page.

Easy Peasy

Map out serving plates. Trace around a clear glass plate onto map paper; cut out paper. Brush decoupage medium onto right side of paper; let set a minute to soften. Center plate on paper, press, then turn over. Gently press paper onto back side of plate, working from center to edge. Let decoupage medium dry. For flag picks in cupcakes, use the pattern on page 156 to cut flags from map paper. Tape straight end to a toothpick then tightly roll partway.

Grad Year Vase

Recycle a clean container, such as one from shortening or oats, to make a vase. Cut map paper to fit container. Use double-sided tape to hold paper in place. Carefully mold a metal label holder to container. Cut paper to fit holder. Press number stickers onto paper for graduation year; chalk edges black. Use double-stick tape to adhere label to container. Hot-glue holder over label. Tie ribbon around container top. Line vase with a plastic container before filling with water.

Clever Cones

Cardboard cones make snappy favors. To cover with map paper, tape a straight edge of paper vertically on cone. Wrap cone with paper. Trim off excess, leaving an inch to tuck over top. Tape paper edge in place. Use a plastic triangle decorator bag to line, then add munchies.

Traveling Around

Greet party guests with a wreath to set the journey theme. Trace patterns, page 156, then cut out. Use the large pattern to cut out 14 shapes from map paper. Cut out 14 diamonds from light green card stock. Overlap the edges of the large pieces as shown in the illustrations (page 156); tape. Fold up the tips as shown on the illustration. Fold diamonds in half as indicated. Use a piece of double-sided tape to adhere shapes to an 18-inch flat wreath form. Hot-glue the diamonds between the large pieces, as shown below.

See the World

Spark travel conversations with mini globes nested atop colorful candleholders. Hot-glue the orbs in place then cluster the decorations as accent pieces.

Cargo Card Box

A small rigid suitcase or storage box will hold cards and small graduation gifts. Using the box design as a guide, cut map pieces to fit top and sides. Brush the back of each map piece with decoupage medium to adhere pieces in place. Place a note by the box that reads, "stow away grad cards here" for guests to leave their greetings.

Mapped Out

It's tradition to share photos from all ages at graduation parties. Small photos, placed here and there as accents, especially in map-decorated frames, unify the theme. Use decoupage medium to attach map strips to frame recesses. Place map paper behind photos as mats, or apply stickers with an initial of the graduate.

Birds of a Feather

Paper or papier mâché, these feathered friends make springtime decorating more fun than ever.

Winged Flair

A simple childhood craft soars above elementary. This fashion-forward tabletop accent brings coos of delight.

WHAT YOU NEED

egg
large needle
newspapers
lightweight cardboard
masking tape
crafts glue
sandpaper
white paint
paintbrush

WHAT YOU DO

1. Polk a hole in the ends of a raw egg using large needle; gently blow out the insides. Let dry.

2. Ball newspaper into a head shape; attach to clean eggshell using masking tape. Cut tail and wings from lightweight cardboard, such as a cereal box. Use masking tape to attach pieces to eggshell, as shown in Photo A.

3. Mix equal parts glue and water. Tear newspaper into strips; soak strips in the mixture. Run each strip through your fingers to coat and remove excess glue. Layer strips over bird to cover, as shown in Photo B.

4. Let dry 24 hours or until dry to the touch. Sand smooth. Paint white. When dry, add a second coat if necessary.

Feather Pillow

A bird-theme image is sophisticated. Turn a photo into a custom-made pillow for a designer look—minus the price tag.

WHAT YOU NEED

digital image
iron-on transfer paper
iron
cotton pillow cover

WHAT YOU DO

1. Print image on iron-on transfer paper. For large images, tile the photo using several sheets of transfer paper. Let dry.

2. Trim the printed image as shown in Photo A, and lay it facedown on a cotton pillow cover. Iron, with a dry iron, pressing firmly and moving the iron constantly, as shown in Photo B.

3. Lift a corner to see if the image has transferred, as shown in Photo C. When image has transferred to pillow cover, carefully peel off backing. For tiled images, protect finished portions from excess heat with a used piece of transfer paper as shown in Photo C.

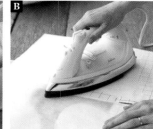

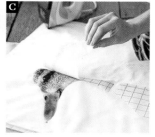

Easy Does It
Nesting In

Natural Winner

Make an egg-laden nest the focal point of a twig wreath by keeping the arrangement simple. Wire a large nest into a twig wreath. Paint three wooden eggs light blue; hot-glue to the nest. Finish the wreath with a large ribbon bow peeking over the nest.

Proudly Perched

A miniature nest, tiny bird, and pea-size eggs rolled from oven-bake crafting clay make this napkin ring super special. Hot-glue the arrangement to a wooden napkin ring and get ready to amaze your guests. For a tasty option, replace the clay eggs with small wrapped candy eggs.

Pretty Place Card

Sprigs of artificial foliage along with a few twig snippets feather this nest to display a banner-style place card. Hot-glue the pieces in place or leave them loose to swap out for every season.

Blooming Pedestal

Despite their delicate appearance, grape hyacinths are hardy enough to use in live arrangements. Enjoy their spring-fresh cheer for days, watering lightly daily, then plant outdoors before summer. Tuck moss around stems. Place arrangement in a footed tiered dish.

Beribboned Beauty

A trio of gingham ribbon bows coordinates with colorful candies. Line a crafts-store twig nest with a clear glass bowl and tie bows around the twigs.

ASPARAGUS IN
MUSTARD-DILL SAUCE
PAGE 73

food

GATHER ROUND

At any celebration special foods tempt guests to the table. Bring family and friends together with recipes for good times—from an Easter feast to the perfect potluck lasagna.

CLASSIC DEVILED EGGS
PAGE 77

Chocolate Bliss

Melt someone's heart with these warm, gooey chocolate desserts, perfect for sharing in the sweetest way.

CHOCOLATE-FILLED RED VELVET CUPCAKES

Chocolate-Filled Red Velvet Cupcakes

PREP 25 minutes FREEZE 1 hour
BAKE 15 minutes at 375°F
COOL 10 minutes

WHAT YOU NEED

1 cup milk chocolate pieces
¼ cup whipping cream
¼ cup plus 1 tablespoon butter
1 egg
1 cup all-purpose flour
2 teaspoons unsweetened cocoa powder
¼ teaspoon salt
¾ cup sugar
2 teaspoons red food coloring
½ teaspoon vanilla
½ cup buttermilk
½ teaspoon baking soda
½ teaspoon vinegar
   Raspberry preserves (optional)

WHAT YOU DO

1. For truffle filling, in a small saucepan combine chocolate pieces, cream, and the 1 tablespoon butter. Stir over low heat until chocolate is melted. Transfer to a small bowl; cool for 15 minutes, stirring occasionally. Cover and freeze about 1 hour, until a fudgelike consistency. Divide filling in 12 portions. Working quickly with hands, roll each portion in a ball. Place truffles in freezer.
2. Meanwhile, let ¼ cup butter and egg stand at room temperature for 30 minutes. Preheat oven to 375°F. Line 12 (2½-inch) muffin cups with paper bake cups. Set aside.
3. For batter, in a small bowl stir together flour, cocoa powder, and salt. In a mixing bowl beat the ¼ cup butter with mixer on medium for 30 seconds. Gradually add sugar; beat on medium to combine. Beat on medium 2 minutes more, scraping bowl occasionally. Beat in egg, food coloring, and vanilla. Alternately add flour mixture and buttermilk, beating on low after each addition just until combined. In a small bowl combine baking soda and vinegar; stir into batter.
4. Divide half of the batter among the prepared cups, partially filling the cups. Center a frozen truffle on top of batter in each cup away from sides of cups. Spoon the remaining batter into cups, covering the truffles.
5. Bake for 15 to 18 minutes, until tops spring back when lightly touched. Remove from oven. Cool 10 minutes. Serve warm, topped with raspberry preserves, if desired. Makes 12 cupcakes.

MALTED MILK BALL CAKE

Malted Milk Ball Cake

PREP 30 minutes
BAKE 25 minutes at 350°F

WHAT YOU NEED

2 cups all-purpose flour
½ cup unsweetened cocoa powder
1 teaspoon baking powder
½ teaspoon baking soda
½ teaspoon salt
⅔ cup butter, softened
1¾ cups sugar
3 eggs
4 ounces unsweetened chocolate, melted and cooled
2 teaspoons vanilla
1½ cups milk
1 cup malted milk balls, coarsely chopped
1 recipe Chocolate Malt Glaze (see recipe, right)

WHAT YOU DO

1. Line two 9×9×2-inch baking pans with parchment paper. Greast pans; set aside.
2. In a medium bowl stir together the flour, cocoa powder, baking powder, baking soda, and salt. Set aside.
3. Preheat oven to 350°F. In a large mixing bowl beat the butter with electric mixer on medium-high for 30 seconds. Add sugar; beat until combined. Add eggs, one at a time, beating 30 seconds after each. Beat in chocolate and vanilla. Alternately add flour mixture and milk, beating on low after each addition until thoroughly combined.
4. Divide batter between prepared pans; spread evenly. Bake for 10 to 15 minutes. Sprinkle with malted milk balls, pressing in slightly if needed (see Tip below). Continue baking 10 to 15 minutes more (25 minutes total baking time).
5. Let cakes stand on wire racks while preparing Chocolate Malt Glaze. Spread warm cake with warm glaze. Makes 24 servings.
TIP: For candy to keep its shape and crunch, partially bake the cakes until nearly set. Press in chopped balls, then continue baking for the remaining time.
Chocolate Malt Glaze: In a medium microwave-safe bowl, whisk together ⅔ cup whipping cream and ⅓ cup malted milk powder. Microwave on 50% power (medium) for 2 minutes or until bubbly. Place one 11.5-ounce package milk chocolate pieces in another medium heat-proof bowl; pour hot whipping cream mixture over chocolate pieces. Let stand 5 minutes; stir. Use immediately.

WARM CHOCOLATE GRAVY

CHOCOLATE-RASPBERRY GRILLERS

Chocolate-Raspberry Grillers

START TO FINISH **18 minutes**

WHAT YOU NEED

8 ½-inch-thick slices challah or Hawaiian sweet bread
2 tablespoons butter, melted
4 to 6 ounces semisweet chocolate, finely chopped
1 cup raspberries
Warm Chocolate Gravy (see recipe, right)

WHAT YOU DO

1. Heat a large heavy nonstick skillet over medium-low heat. Meanwhile, brush one side of each bread slice with some of the melted butter. Place half the bread slices, buttered side down, on a plate. Sprinkle with chocolate and raspberries to within ¼ inch of crusts. Top with remaining bread, buttered sides up. Place sandwiches, two at a time, in skillet. Weight with a heavy skillet.
2. Grill two sandwiches at a time over medium-low heat for 6 to 8 minutes, until chocolate is melted and bread is golden brown, turning once midway through grilling time. Grill remaining sandwiches.
3. Slice sandwiches in half to serve. Pass warm Chocolate Gravy for dipping. Makes 8 servings.

Warm Chocolate Gravy

Serve this thick yet light chocolate sauce alongside Chocolate-Raspberry Grillers, or try it over French toast.

START TO FINISH **10 minutes**

WHAT YOU NEED

¼ cup sugar
2 tablespoons unsweetened cocoa powder
1 tablespoon all-purpose flour
1 tablespoon butter
1¼ cups milk

WHAT YOU DO

1. In a small bowl stir together sugar, cocoa powder, and flour. In a medium saucepan melt the butter. Thoroughly stir in sugar mixture until no lumps remain. Gradually add milk, stirring constantly. Cook and stir over medium heat until thickened and bubbly; cook and stir 1 minute more. Serve with Chocolate-Raspberry Grillers.

TIP: Cover and refrigerate any remaining gravy up to 2 days. To reheat ½ to ⅔ cup gravy, place in a microwave-safe bowl. Heat at 100% power (high) for 1 to 2 minutes, just until heated through, stirring once. Or place the gravy in a small saucepan and warm over medium-low heat, stirring constantly. Makes 10 servings.

Gooey Chocolate Pudding Cakes

PREP **20 minutes**
BAKE **20 minutes at 350°F**

WHAT YOU NEED

½ cup all-purpose flour
¼ cup sugar
¾ teaspoon baking powder
¼ teaspoon salt
⅓ cup milk
1 tablespoon oil
1 teaspoon vanilla
¼ cup chocolate-hazelnut spread (Nutella)
⅓ cup semisweet chocolate pieces
½ cup sugar
¼ cup unsweetened cocoa powder
¾ cup boiling water
 Coffee-flavored or vanilla ice cream (optional)
 Sliced strawberries (optional)
 Unsweetened cocoa powder (optional)

WHAT YOU DO

1. Preheat oven to 350°F. In a medium bowl combine flour, the ¼ cup sugar, baking powder, and salt. Add milk, oil, and vanilla. Whisk until smooth. Stir in chocolate-hazelnut spread and semisweet chocolate pieces.
2. Divide batter evenly among six 5- to 8-ounce oven-safe bowls or ramekins. Place in a 15×10×1-inch baking pan. Set aside. In the same bowl for the batter, stir together ½ cup sugar and cocoa. Gradually stir in boiling water. Pour evenly over batter in dishes.
3. Bake, uncovered, for 20 minutes or until a wooden toothpick inserted into cake portion comes out clean. Serve warm with ice cream and strawberries, if desired. Sprinkle with additional cocoa powder. Makes 6 servings.

GOOEY CHOCOLATE
PUDDING CAKES

DOUBLE-CHOCOLATE BREAD
PUDDING WITH STRAWBERRY
SAUCE

Double-Chocolate Bread Pudding with Strawberry Sauce

PREP 35 minutes SLOW COOK 2 hours 30 minutes COOL 30 minutes

WHAT YOU NEED

    Nonstick cooking spray
3   cups whole milk
1   cup sugar
¼   cup butter
1   cup semisweet chocolate pieces
⅔   cup unsweetened cocoa powder
1   tablespoon vanilla
4   eggs, lightly beaten
6   cups dry ¾-inch Italian bread cubes (see Tip, below)
1   16-ounce container frozen sliced strawberries in syrup, thawed
⅓   cup strawberry preserves

WHAT YOU DO

1. Lightly coat the inside of a 3½- or 4-quart slow cooker with cooking spray. Set cooker aside.
2. In a medium saucepan heat milk, sugar, and butter over medium heat until very warm but not boiling, stirring occasionally to dissolve sugar. Remove from heat. Add chocolate pieces and cocoa powder (do not stir); let stand for 5 minutes. Add vanilla. Whisk until smooth; cool slightly (about 10 minutes).
3. In an extra-large mixing bowl, whisk together eggs and chocolate mixture. Gently stir in bread cubes. Transfer pudding to prepared cooker.
4. Cover and cook on low about 2½ hours or until pudding is puffed and seems set when gently shaken. Turn off cooker. If possible, remove crockery liner from cooker and place on wire rack. Cool, uncovered, for 30 minutes (pudding will fall slightly as it cools).
5. Meanwhile, to make strawberry sauce, in a blender or food processor, puree strawberries with syrup and strawberry preserves until smooth. Cover; refrigerate until serving.
6. To serve, spoon warm pudding into dessert dishes and serve with the strawberry sauce. Makes 8 servings.
TIP: To make dried bread cubes, cut a soft supermarket Italian bread loaf (not crusty) into ¾-inch cubes to equal 6 cups (about 9 ounces of bread). Spread bread cubes evenly in a 15×10×1-inch baking pan. Bake, uncovered, in a 300°F oven for 10 to 15 minutes or until cubes are dry, stirring twice. Cool.

Warm Chocolate-Swirl Vanilla Rice Pudding

A swirl of rich chocolate sauce made with a bit of molasses adds extra flavor to this creamy home-style dessert. If you prefer, substitute dark corn syrup for the molasses

PREP 25 minutes
BAKE 45 minutes at 325°F

WHAT YOU NEED

3   eggs, lightly beaten
2   cups half-and-half, light cream, or whole milk
½   cup milk
½   cup sugar
1   teaspoon vanilla or ½ teaspoon almond extract
1   cup cooked white rice, cooled
1   cup sugar
3   tablespoons unsweetened cocoa powder
1   1-ounce square semisweet or bittersweet chocolate, finely chopped
⅛   teaspoon salt
⅓   cup water
1   tablespoon molasses
½   teaspoon vanilla
    Lingonberry sauce (optional)
    Sweetened whipped cream

WHAT YOU DO

1. Preheat oven to 325°F. For rice pudding, in a large mixing bowl beat together the eggs, half-and-half, milk, the ½ cup sugar, and vanilla with a rotary beater or wire whisk. Stir in rice. Pour into a 1½- or 2-quart oval baking dish. Place dish in a roasting pan set on a rack. Carefully pour 1 inch of boiling water into the baking pan. Bake, uncovered, for 45 to 50 minutes, until a knife inserted near center comes out clean.
2. Meanwhile, for chocolate sauce, in a small saucepan stir together the 1 cup sugar, cocoa powder, chopped chocolate, and salt. Stir in water. Cook and stir over medium heat until chocolate is dissolved and the sauce comes to a simmer. Remove from heat. Stir in molasses and the ½ teaspoon vanilla. Transfer sauce to a serving bowl; cover with plastic wrap.
3. As soon as rice pudding is removed from oven, stir and swirl in some of the chocolate sauce. Serve rice pudding warm with lingonberry sauce, if desired, and sweetened whipped cream. Pass remaining chocolate sauce. Makes 8 servings.

Easy Easter Feast

Glazed ham, simple sides, make-ahead rolls, and a pastel sherbet cake for dessert make this celebratory springtime meal enjoyable for everyone—especially the cook!

Garlic- and Pineapple-Glazed Ham

Just a few ingredients—fresh pineapple and pineapple juice, honey, and crushed red pepper—turn a simple ham into a special occasion. Making the sauce is as simple as opening a jar of your favorite mustard. Grainy country-style Dijon is always nice.

PREP **15 minutes** BAKE **2 hours 15 minutes at 325°F**

WHAT YOU NEED
1   6 to 8-pound cooked ham, rump half
1   cup chopped fresh pineapple
¼   cup honey
8   to 10 cloves garlic, minced
1   teaspoon crushed red pepper
2   to 4 tablespoons unsweetened pineapple juice (optional)
    Fresh pineapple wedges (optional)
    Desired mustard (optional)

WHAT YOU DO
1. Preheat oven to 325°F. If desired, score ham in a diamond pattern by making shallow diagonal cuts at 1-inch intervals.
2. Place ham on a rack in a shallow roasting pan. Insert an oven-going meat thermometer into center of ham. The thermometer should not touch bone. Cover with foil; bake for 1½ hours.
3. Meanwhile, for glaze, in a food processor or blender combine 1 cup pineapple, honey, garlic, and crushed red pepper. Cover and process or blend until nearly smooth.
4. Brush ham generously with glaze. Bake, uncovered, for 45 to 60 minutes more or until thermometer registers 140°F. If desired, drizzle ham with pineapple juice to moisten. If desired, garnish with pineapple wedges and serve with mustard. Makes 20 servings.
Variation: Instead of pineapple, use canned apricots or peaches. Substitute maple syrup for the honey.

GARLIC- AND PINEAPPLE-
GLAZED HAM

ASPARAGUS IN
MUSTARD-DILL SAUCE

Asparagus in Mustard-Dill Sauce

PREP **10 minutes**
BAKE **15 minutes at 425°F**

WHAT YOU NEED
4   pounds asparagus spears
½   cup reduced-sodium chicken broth
¼   cup dill mustard
¼   cup finely shredded Parmesan or Asiago cheese
    Coarsely ground black pepper

WHAT YOU DO
1. Preheat oven to 425°F. Snap off and discard woody bases from asparagus. Arrange asparagus in a 3-quart rectangular baking dish. In a small bowl combine broth and mustard. Pour over asparagus, turning to coat.
2. Bake for 15 to 20 minutes or until asparagus is crisp-tender. Transfer to a serving dish. Sprinkle with cheese and pepper. Makes 8 servings.

OVERNIGHT
REFRIGERATOR ROLLS

Overnight Refrigerator Rolls

PREP **35 minutes** CHILL **overnight**
RISE **45 minutes**
BAKE **12 minutes at 375°F**

WHAT YOU NEED
1¼ cups warm water (105°F to 115°F)
1   package active dry yeast
4   to 4¼ cups all-purpose flour
⅓   cup butter, melted, or vegetable oil
⅓   cup sugar
1   teaspoon salt
1   egg
     Nonstick cooking spray

WHAT YOU NEED
1. In a large mixing bowl combine warm water and yeast. Stir to dissolve yeast. Add 1½ cups of the flour, melted butter, sugar, salt, and egg. Beat with an electric mixer on low speed for 1 minute, scraping sides of bowl constantly.
2. Using a wooden spoon, stir in enough of the remaining flour to make a soft dough that just starts to pull away from sides of bowl (dough will be slightly sticky). Coat a 3-quart covered container with cooking spray. Place dough in container; turn once to grease surface of dough. Cover and refrigerate overnight.
3. Punch dough down. Turn dough out onto a lightly floured surface. Divide dough in half. Cover and let rest for 10 minutes. Meanwhile, lightly grease a 13×9×2-inch baking pan or baking sheets.
4. Shape dough into 24 balls or rolls (don't overwork dough; it becomes more sticky the more you work with it) and place in prepared baking pan or 2 to 3 inches apart on baking sheets. Cover; let rise in a warm place until nearly double in size (about 45 minutes).
5. Preheat oven to 375°F. Bake for 12 to 15 minutes for individual rolls or about 20 minutes for pan rolls or until golden. Immediately remove rolls from pans. Serve warm. Makes 24 rolls.
Butterhorn Rolls: On a lightly floured surface, roll each dough half into a 10-inch circle. If desired, brush with melted butter or margarine. Cut each dough circle into 12 wedges. To shape rolls, begin at wide end of each wedge and loosely roll toward the point. Place, point sides down, 2 to 3 inches apart on prepared baking sheets. Makes 24 rolls.
Rosettes: Divide each dough half into 16 pieces. On a lightly floured surface,

roll each piece into a 12-inch-long rope. Tie each rope in a loose knot, leaving two long ends. Tuck top end under knot and bottom end into the top center. Place 2 to 3 inches apart on prepared baking sheets. Makes 32 rolls.
Parker House Rolls: On a lightly floured surface, roll each dough half to ¼-inch thickness. Cut dough with a floured 2½-inch round cutter. Brush with melted butter or margarine. Using the dull edge of a table knife, make an off-center crease in each round. Fold each round along the crease. Press folded edge firmly. Place, large half up, 2 to 3 inches apart on prepared baking sheets. Makes 24 rolls.

Browned Butter-Green Onion New Potatoes

PREP **20 minutes**
ROAST **30 minutes at 425°F**

WHAT YOU NEED
3   pounds tiny new potatoes, halved, or medium round red or white potatoes, cut into eighths

BROWNED BUTTER-GREEN ONION NEW POTATOES

3   tablespoons olive oil
1   teaspoon kosher salt
½   teaspoon garlic powder
½   teaspoon ground black pepper
¼   cup butter
⅓   cup thinly sliced green onions
3   tablespoons packed brown sugar
     Kosher or coarse salt

WHAT YOU DO
1. Preheat oven to 425°F. Place potatoes in a shallow roasting pan. In a small bowl combine oil, 1 teaspoon salt, the garlic powder, and pepper. Drizzle oil mixture over potatoes, tossing to coat. Roast, uncovered, for 20 minutes, stirring once.
2. Meanwhile, in a small saucepan melt butter over low heat. Continue heating until butter turns a light golden brown. Remove from heat; set aside.
3. Stir potatoes. Stir in browned butter, green onions, and brown sugar. Roast, uncovered, for 10 to 15 minutes more or until potatoes are tender and lightly browned. Sprinkle lightly with additional kosher salt to serve. Makes 10 to 12 servings.

CLASSIC DEVILED EGGS

Classic Deviled Eggs

START TO FINISH **30 minutes**

WHAT YOU NEED
6 hard-cooked eggs (see Tip, below)
2 tablespoons mayonnaise
2 tablespoons low-fat plain
   Greek yogurt
1 teaspoon vinegar
½ teaspoon mustard
   Paprika for garnish

WHAT YOU DO
1. Peel eggs. Cut in half lengthwise and remove yolks. Set whites aside.
2. In a small bowl, mash yolks with a fork. Add mayonnaise, yogurt, vinegar, and mustard; mix well.
3. Stuff egg white halves with yolk mixture. Cover and chill until serving time, up to 24 hours. Makes 12 servings.
TIP: To hard-cook eggs, place eggs in a single layer in a large saucepan (do not stack eggs). Add enough cold water to cover eggs by 1 inch. Bring to a rapid boil over high heat (water will have large rapidly breaking bubbles). Remove from heat, cover, and let stand for 15 minutes; drain. Run cold water over the eggs or place them in ice water until cool enough to handle; drain. To peel eggs, gently tap each egg on the countertop. Roll the egg between the palms of your hands. Peel off eggshell, starting at the large end.
Bacon and Cheese: Mash four of the yolks. (Save extras to toss in a salad.) Add ½ cup finely shredded cheddar and four slices of crumbled bacon to the yolk filling. Garnish with fresh chives instead of paprika.
Edamame: Mash four of the yolks. Add ½ cup chilled, pureed edamame to the filling. Garnish with whole edamame instead of paprika.

LAYERED
SHERBET CAKE

Layered Sherbet Cake

PREP **1 hour** COOL **1 hour**
FREEZE **4 hours** STAND **10 minutes**

WHAT YOU NEED
1 package 2-layer-size white or yellow cake mix
2 cups orange sherbet, softened
2 cups lime sherbet, softened
2 cups raspberry sherbet, softened
1 8-ounce package cream cheese, softened
½ cup powdered sugar
¼ cup milk
1 teaspoon vanilla
1 16-ounce container frozen whipped dessert topping, thawed
   Small decorative candies or multicolor sprinkles

WHAT YOU DO
1. Prepare, bake, and cool cake as directed for 8-inch layers.
2. Using a long serrated knife, cut each cake layer in half horizontally. Place one cake layer*, cut side up, in an 8-inch springform pan (if necessary, trim to fit). Attach sides of pan. Spoon orange sherbet onto cake layer in pan; spread evenly. Top with second cake layer; spread with lime sherbet. Top with third cake layer; spread with raspberry sherbet. Top with fourth cake layer, cut side down. Cover with plastic wrap; freeze for 3 to 4 hours or until firm.
3. For frosting, in a large mixing bowl beat cream cheese, powdered sugar, milk, and vanilla with an electric mixer on medium to high speed until light and fluffy. Stir in a small amount of the whipped topping to lighten. Fold in the remaining whipped topping.
4. Remove plastic wrap from cake. Remove sides of pan. Using a wide spatula, transfer cake from springform pan to a serving plate. Spread top and sides of cake with frosting. Top cake with small candies. Freeze, uncovered, for 1 to 2 hours or until firm.
5. Let stand at room temperature for 10 to 15 minutes before serving. Cut into wedges. Makes 16 servings.
TIP: Because the split cake layers are thin, place the first layer on the bottom of the springform pan before attaching the sides of the pan to prevent the layer from breaking. Set the last cake layer on top of the sherbet, gently pressing the cake to seal it to the sherbet.

SHOOTING STAR
COOKIES
PAGE 80

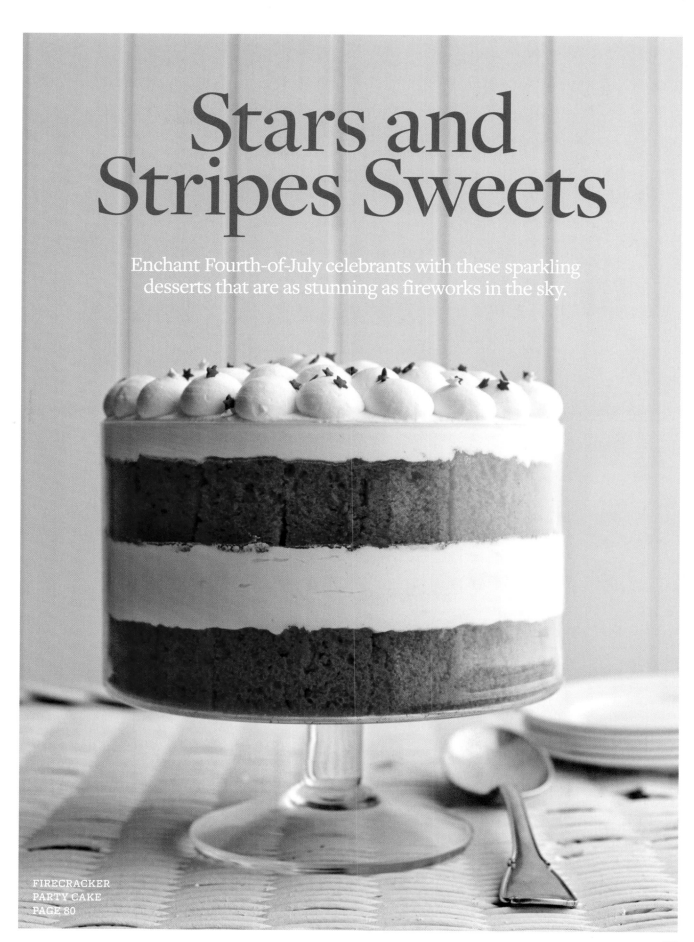

Stars and Stripes Sweets

Enchant Fourth-of-July celebrants with these sparkling desserts that are as stunning as fireworks in the sky.

FIRECRACKER
PARTY CAKE
PAGE 80

Shooting Star Cookies

shown on page 78

PREP 1 hour 30 minutes
CHILL 1 hour 10 minutes
BAKE 10 minutes at 325°F
STAND 10 minutes

WHAT YOU NEED
Plain Dough
1   cup unsalted butter, softened
1   cup granulated sugar
2   eggs
3   cups all-purpose flour
1   teaspoon salt
1   teaspoon vanilla bean paste or
    vanilla extract

Blue Dough
1   cup unsalted butter, softened
1   cup granulated sugar
2   eggs
3   cups all-purpose flour
1   teaspoon salt
1   teaspoon vanilla bean paste or
    vanilla extract
¼   teaspoon blue color gel or
    1 tablespoon liquid food coloring
    Royal Icing (see recipe, page 147)

WHAT YOU DO
1. For Plain Dough, in bowl of a stand mixer combine butter and sugar. Beat on high until light and fluffy. Scrape down bottom and sides of bowl. Add eggs, one at a time, beating well after each addition.
2. In a bowl whisk flour and salt. With mixer on low, add vanilla to butter mixture. Gradually add flour mixture. Transfer to plastic wrap; press into a rectangle. Wrap; chill 20 minutes.
3. For Blue Dough, follow Step 1, beating butter, sugar, and eggs. In a medium bowl whisk together flour and salt. With mixer on low, add vanilla and blue gel to butter mixture. Gradually add flour mixture until combined. Transfer to plastic wrap; press into a rectangle. Wrap; chill 20 minutes. Prepare Royal Icing.
4. Divide each dough in half. Roll each piece into a 12×8-inch rectangle. Transfer to plastic wrap. Invert a blue rectangle on plain rectangle; remove top piece of plastic or paper. Invert remaining plain rectangle on stack; remove plastic or paper. Add remaining blue rectangle; remove plastic or paper. Cut into four 8×3-inch strips. Stack strips on one another; press to adhere (16 layers). Wrap and chill 30 minutes or up to 1½ hours.

5. Preheat oven to 325°F. Using a sharp knife, trim short end of stack. Cut ¼-inch slice from short end. Press slice to about ¼-inch thickness. Using a 3-inch star-shape cutter, cut star from slice. Transfer to parchment-lined baking sheet. Repeat with remaining stack (makes about 28 striped stars). Gather scraps; pat together. Reroll to ¼-inch thickness. Dough will be marbled. Cut 3-inch stars. Transfer to baking sheet. Using 1¼-inch star cutter, cut stars from centers of 14 marbled stars.
6. Bake 10 to 12 minutes. While warm, recut cookies with clean 3-inch cutter to ensure cookies align when assembled. Cool on wire racks.
7. Place half the striped cookies top sides down; pipe a thin ribbon of Royal Icing around edges. Place marbled cookies with cutouts on top; align edges. Let dry 2 minutes. Spoon red sugar into cutout. Pipe a strip of icing along edge of each. Top with striped cookies, top sides up. Let stand 10 minutes. Makes 14 sandwich cookies and 22 marbled cookies.

Firecracker Party Cake

shown on page 79

PREP 25 minutes BAKE 20 minutes at 350°F COOL 1 hour
FREEZE 30 minutes STAND 15 minutes
CHILL 2 hours 30 minutes

WHAT YOU NEED
6   eggs, separated
    Nonstick baking spray
1   cup sugar
3   tablespoons water
3   tablespoons canola oil
1½ teaspoons red color gel or
    1 tablespoon red liquid food color
1   teaspoon cinnamon oil
1   cup cake flour
1   teaspoon baking powder
¼   teaspoon cayenne pepper
1   teaspoon salt
1   teaspoon cream of tartar
½   cup water
1   teaspoon unflavored gelatin
3½ cups whipping cream
1   8-ounce container mascarpone
    cheese
1   cup powdered sugar

WHAT YOU DO
1. Allow separated eggs to come to room temperature. Preheat oven to 350°F. Coat

a 15×10×1-inch baking pan with nonstick spray for baking; line bottom of pan with parchment. Set aside.
2. For cake, in a large bowl whisk together egg yolks, ¼ cup of the sugar, the 3 tablespoons water, 3 tablespoons canola oil, food coloring, and cinnamon oil.
3. In a bowl whisk cake flour, baking powder, and cayenne. Sift flour mixture over egg yolk mixture; stir. Set aside.
4. In a separate bowl of a stand mixer combine egg whites and salt. Beat on high until foamy. Sprinkle in cream of tartar. Beat 10 seconds. Add remaining ¾ cup sugar. Beat on high until stiff peaks form.
5. Stir about half the egg whites into egg yolk mixture. Fold remaining egg whites into egg yolk mixture. Spoon batter into prepared pan. Bake 20 minutes or until a toothpick inserted near center comes out clean. Cool in pan on a wire rack 10 minutes. Loosen sides, invert cake onto a wire rack and remove parchment. Cool completely. Wrap in plastic wrap. Freeze for 30 minutes.
6. Using a long serrated knife, cut cake into 1½-inch-wide strips. Cut strips crosswise into 1½-inch squares. Set aside.
7. Place the ½ cup water in a small microwave-safe bowl. Sprinkle gelatin over. Let stand 5 minutes. Microwave at 10-second intervals until gelatin is melted, swirling after each interval. Let stand 10 minutes.
8. For frosting, in the large bowl of a stand mixer combine whipping cream, mascarpone, and powdered sugar. Beat until soft peaks form. Stir a dollop of cream mixture into gelatin mixture. With mixer running, slowly add gelatin mixture to frosting. Beat on high until stiff peaks form. Transfer to large pastry bag fitted with a large round tip.
9. To assemble, line inner edge of a 4- to 5-quart clear glass straight-side bowl or trifle dish with cake pieces, pressing pieces close together with no gaps. Fill center with cake pieces in an even layer. Pipe or spread an even 1½-inch layer of frosting on cake. Arrange a second layer of cake on frosting. Evenly pipe or spread another layer of frosting to top of bowl. Starting around edge and working toward center, pipe small mounds of frosting. Top with sprinkles. Cover; chill for 2½ hours or up to 24 hours before serving. Makes 20 servings.

Frozen Yogurt Icebox Cake

Let the dessert stand a few minutes before serving. You'll get fuller flavor and creamier texture, and it's easier to slice. Eat it right after serving—it will start to melt quickly!

PREP **45 minutes**
FREEZE **37 hours** STAND **10 minutes**

WHAT YOU NEED
   Nonstick cooking spray
2 pints low-fat vanilla-flavor Greek frozen yogurt
2 pints low-fat strawberry-flavor Greek frozen yogurt
¼ cup pomegranate or cherry juice
2 teaspoons red color gel or 4½ teaspoons red liquid food color
2 pints low-fat blueberry-flavor Greek frozen yogurt
¼ cup blueberry juice
½ teaspoon blue color gel or 1½ teaspoons liquid food color
   Coconut chips, crushed

WHAT YOU DO
1. For stars, place frozen vanilla yogurt in a chilled bowl; stir to soften. Coat six cavities of a silicone star-shape mini treat mold with nonstick cooking spray. Completely fill cavities with softened yogurt, about ⅓ cup each. Freeze until solid, about 12 hours. Freeze any remaining yogurt; save for another use.
2. In a large chilled bowl combine strawberry frozen yogurt and pomegranate juice. Stir to soften. Add red food coloring. Cover; freeze 1 hour or until mixture is spreadable.
3. In a large chilled bowl combine blueberry frozen yogurt and blueberry juice. Stir to soften. Add blue food coloring. Cover; freeze 1 hour or until mixture is spreadable.
4. Line a 9-inch Pullman or loaf pan with two sheets of plastic wrap large enough to cover bottom and sides and extend over sides of pan. Spread red yogurt evenly in bottom of pan. Remove stars from mold. Closely arrange along center of red yogurt, pressing so bottom points are completely submerged and tops are just visible. Stars will touch. Freeze 1 hour. Remove from freezer. Spread blue yogurt in an even layer over stars to cover. Freeze until firm, at least 24 hours.
5. To remove, use plastic wrap to lift cake from pan. Transfer to a serving plate; sprinkle with coconut chips. Let stand 10 minutes; slice. Wrap and refreeze any remaining cake. Makes 10 servings.

FROZEN YOGURT ICEBOX CAKE

Berry Flag Tart

PREP **2 hours**
BAKE **1 hour 15 minutes at 350°F**

WHAT YOU NEED
Crust
3   cups all-purpose flour
2   tablespoons granulated sugar
1½ teaspoons salt
1½ cups cold unsalted butter, cut into
       ½-inch slices
½   cup ice water
1   egg
⅓   cup Swedish (pearl) sugar

Fillings
5   6-ounce packages fresh
       raspberries (8 cups)
3   teaspoons finely shredded lemon
       peel
3   tablespoons lemon juice
1   cup granulated sugar
6   tablespoons ClearJel or
       cornstarch
       Salt
2   6-ounce packages fresh
       blueberries (2 cups)

WHAT YOU DO

1. For crust, in a food processor combine flour, sugar, and salt. Pulse to distribute ingredients. Add butter; pulse until mixture resembles coarse cornmeal with

a few large butter chunks visible. While pulsing, slowly add water. Pulse until water is evenly distributed (don't allow dough to form a ball). Remove dough. Gently knead to incorporate any remaining dry bits. Divide into two portions, one portion with about two-thirds of the dough (1 ounce). Wrap each in plastic wrap. Chill 30 minutes.
2. Roll large portion of dough to a 17×12-inch rectangle. Transfer to a 15×10×1-inch baking pan. Press dough up sides of pan; trim edges. Prick bottom of dough. Chill. Roll remaining dough into a 15×10-inch rectangle about ¼ inch thick. Cut lengthwise into six ½-inch-wide strips. Cut four ½-inch strips 9 inches long. Cut 1-inch stars from remaining

BERRY FLAG
TART

COCONUT CREAM
ISLAND PUNCH

dough, rerolling scraps. Place stripes and stars on a parchment-lined baking sheet. Brush with mixture of egg and 1 tablespoon water. Sprinkle with Swedish sugar; press into dough. Chill.
3. For raspberry filling, place raspberries in a large bowl. Toss with 2 teaspoons lemon peel and 2 tablespoons juice, ¾ cup sugar, 4 tablespoons ClearJel, and a pinch of salt. Stir to coat. Set aside.
4. For blueberry filling, place blueberries in a large bowl. Toss with 1 teaspoon lemon peel and 1 tablespoon juice. In a small bowl combine the remaining ¼ cup sugar, 2 tablespoons ClearJel, and a pinch of salt. Stir to coat. Set aside.
5. Preheat oven to 350°F. With long side of dough-lined pan toward you, arrange blueberry filling in upper left corner, covering a 6×4-inch rectangle. Spoon raspberry filling around blueberries to fill pan. Place dough strips over raspberries, trimming as necessary. Place stars over blueberries. Bake 1¼ hours or until filling bubbles and edges of crust are golden-brown; cool. Makes 24 servings.

Coconut Cream Island Punch

PREP **15 minutes** CHILL **30 minutes**

WHAT YOU NEED
2 large fresh star fruit, thinly sliced (about 1 pound) or 2 cups sliced fresh strawberries
6 cups grapefruit soda
1⅓ cups spiced rum
1 cup coconut sorbet or gelato Fresh or frozen blueberries (optional)

WHAT YOU DO
1. Pack star fruit slices in a large pitcher; set aside. For punch, in another large pitcher combine the soda, rum, and sorbet. Stir until sorbet is nearly melted. Pour enough punch over star fruit to fill pitcher. Reserve any remaining punch to replenish pitcher while serving. Cover; chill 30 minutes. Top with blueberries, if desired. Makes 7½ cups.

Everybody Loves Lasagna

Make-ahead prep, layers of loveliness, and its self-serve feature make lasagna the perfect warm-up food for a fall or winter potluck.

Meatball Lasagna

PREP 30 minutes ROAST 20 minutes at 425°F (peppers) BAKE 20 minutes at 350°F (meatballs); 55 minutes at 375°F (lasagna) STAND 35 minutes

WHAT YOU NEED

¾ 12-ounce jar roasted red peppers
1½ cups soft whole wheat bread crumbs (about 2 slices)
½ cup refrigerated or frozen egg product, (thawed) or 2 eggs lightly beaten
⅓ cup tomato sauce
½ cup snipped fresh basil, or 1 tablespoon dried basil, crushed
¼ cup snipped fresh flat-leaf parsley
½ teaspoon salt
¼ teaspoon ground black pepper
2 pounds lean ground beef
2 medium green sweet peppers, stemmed, seeded, and quartered
6 dried regular or whole wheat lasagna noodles
1½ cups shredded reduced-fat mozzarella cheese (6 ounces)
½ 15-ounce container (¾ cup) light ricotta cheese
¼ cup soft goat cheese (chèvre) or finely shredded Parmesan cheese (1 ounce)
1½ cups purchased light or low-fat tomato basil pasta sauce
   Shredded fresh basil or small fresh basil or oregano leaves (optional)

WHAT YOU DO

1. For meatballs, preheat oven to 350°F. In a large bowl combine roasted red peppers, bread crumbs, egg product, tomato sauce, basil, parsley, salt, and pepper. Add ground beef; mix well. Shape mixture into 48 meatballs. Place on a large foil-lined baking pan. Bake 20 minutes or until done (160°F); set aside.
2. Turn oven to 425°F. Line a large baking sheet with foil. Place sweet pepper quarters, cut sides down, on prepared baking sheet. Roast, uncovered, about 20 minutes or until peppers are charred. Wrap in foil; let stand 20 minutes. Peel skins from pepper quarters. Set aside. Reduce oven temperature to 375°F.
3. Meanwhile, cook lasagna noodles according to package directions. Drain noodles; rinse with cold water. Drain well; set aside. For filling, in a small bowl, stir together 1 cup of the mozzarella cheese, the ricotta cheese, and the goat cheese; set aside.

4. To assemble, spread ½ cup of the pasta sauce in the bottom of a 2-quart rectangular baking dish. Layer two cooked noodles in the dish. Arrange 24 meatballs* in a single layer on noodles in dish. Add two more cooked noodles. Top with the ricotta cheese mixture, spreading evenly. Arrange sweet pepper pieces on ricotta layer. Top with remaining cooked noodles. Spread remaining pasta sauce over noodles.
5. Bake, covered, for 50 minutes. Uncover and sprinkle with the remaining ½ cup mozzarella cheese. Bake, uncovered, for 5 to 10 minutes more or until heated through. Let stand for 15 minutes before serving. If desired, garnish with fresh herbs. Makes 8 servings.
*NOTE: Freeze remaining meatballs for another use.

SPICY TURKEY LASAGNA

Spicy Turkey Lasagna

PREP 20 minutes SLOW COOK 3 hours 45 minutes (low) STAND 10 minutes

WHAT YOU NEED

12 ounces uncooked ground turkey
1 teaspoon dried oregano, crushed
¼ teaspoon crushed red pepper
1 15-ounce carton ricotta cheese
1¾ cups shredded Italian five-cheese blend
1 10-ounce package frozen chopped spinach, thawed and squeezed dry
3½ cups chunky pasta sauce with mushrooms and green pepper
12 no-boil lasagna noodles
½ cup water
¼ to ½ cup shredded mozzarella cheese (1 to 2 ounces)
   Snipped fresh basil or grated Parmesan cheese (optional)
   Chunky pasta sauce with mushrooms and green pepper (optional)

WHAT YOU DO

1. In a nonstick skillet cook turkey over medium-high heat until no longer pink, using a wooden spoon to break up turkey as it cooks. Remove from heat. Stir in oregano and crushed red pepper.
2. In a large bowl combine ricotta cheese, Italian cheese blend, and spinach.
3. To assemble, spread 1 cup of the pasta sauce a 5-quart oval slow cooker. Top with half the noodles, breaking and overlapping as necessary. Add half of turkey mixture, 1 cup of the pasta sauce, and half the water. Spread half the cheese mixture on top. Repeat layers.
4. Cover and cook on low-heat setting for 3¾ hours. Top with the remaining ½ cup pasta sauce and mozzarella cheese. Let lasagna stand, covered, for 10 minutes before serving.
5. To serve, cut lasagna into eight portions. If desired, sprinkle each serving with basil and Parmesan, and serve with additional pasta sauce. Makes 8 servings.

BBQ CHICKEN-
MACARONI AND
CHEESE "LASAGNA"

BBQ Chicken-Macaroni and Cheese "Lasagna"

PREP 30 minutes
BAKE 20 minutes at 375°F

WHAT YOU NEED
4   cups prepared stovetop macaroni and cheese from your favorite recipe
    Nonstick cooking spray
4   ounces sliced provolone cheese
1   16-ounce tub refrigerated honey-hickory barbecue sauce with shredded chicken
1½ cups coarsely crushed cornflakes
2   tablespoons butter, melted

WHAT YOU DO
1. Preheat oven to 375°F. Coat a 2-quart square baking dish with cooking spray.
2. Spread half the macaroni and cheese in the prepared baking dish. Top with half of the provolone cheese. Spread barbecue sauce with chicken over cheese in dish; top with remaining provolone cheese. Spread remaining macaroni and cheese over ingredients in dish.
3. For topping, in a small bowl combine cornflakes and melted butter, stirring to coat evenly. Sprinkle lasagna with topping. Bake, uncovered, for 20 to 25 minutes or until heated through and topping is lightly browned and crisp. Makes 8 servings.

Classic Lasagna

PREP 30 minutes
COOK 15 minutes
BAKE 30 minutes at 375°F
STAND 15 minutes

WHAT YOU NEED
12 dried lasagna noodles
8   ounces ground beef
8   ounces bulk Italian sausage or bulk pork sausage
1   cup chopped onion (1 large)
2   cloves garlic, minced
1   14.5-ounce can diced tomatoes, undrained
1   8-ounce can tomato sauce
1   tablespoon dried Italian seasoning, crushed
1   teaspoon fennel seeds, crushed
¼   teaspoon ground black pepper
1   egg, lightly beaten
1   15-ounce carton ricotta cheese or 2 cups cottage cheese, drained
¼   cup grated Parmesan cheese
1   recipe Bechamel Sauce (see recipe, right)
2   cups shredded mozzarella cheese (8 ounces)
    Grated Parmesan cheese (optional)
    Snipped fresh basil (optional)

WHAT YOU DO
1. Cook lasagna noodles according to package directions; drain. Rinse with cold water; drain again. Place 3 cooked lasagna noodles in a single layer on a sheet of parchment paper or plastic wrap; top with another sheet of plastic wrap and 3 more lasagna noodles. Repeat to layer all the lasagna noodles; set aside.
2. For meat sauce, in a large skillet cook beef, sausage, onion, and garlic over medium-high heat until meat is browned, using a wooden spoon to break up meat as it cooks. Drain off fat. Stir in tomatoes, tomato sauce, Italian seasoning, fennel seeds, and pepper. Bring to boiling; reduce heat. Cover and simmer for 15 minutes, stirring occasionally.
3. For filling, in a medium bowl combine egg, ricotta cheese, and the ¼ cup Parmesan cheese; set aside.
4. Preheat oven to 375°F. Spread about ¼ cup of the meat sauce in an ungreased 3-quart rectangular baking dish (to keep noodles from sticking to baking dish). Arrange three cooked noodles lengthwise on sauce in dish. Spread with one-fourth of the filling. Spoon one-fourth of the Bechamel Sauce over the filling. Top with one-fourth of the remaining meat sauce and one-fourth of the mozzarella cheese. Repeat layers three more times, starting with noodles and ending with mozzarella cheese (make sure the top layer of noodles is evenly covered with sauce). If desired, sprinkle with additional Parmesan cheese.
5. Bake, uncovered, for 30 to 35 minutes or until hot in the center (160°F). Let stand for 15 minutes before serving. If desired, garnish with basil.
Makes 12 servings.
Bechamel Sauce: In a medium saucepan heat 2 tablespoons butter over medium heat until melted. Add 3 cloves garlic, minced; cook and stir for 1 minute (to infuse butter with garlic flavor). Stir in 3 tablespoons all-purpose flour, ¼ teaspoon salt, and ¼ teaspoon ground black pepper until combined. Stir in 2 cups milk all at once. Cook and stir until thickened and bubbly. Cook and stir for 1 minute more. Remove from heat. Stir in ¼ cup grated Parmesan cheese.

CLASSIC LASAGNA

MILE-HIGH LASAGNA PIE

Mile-High Lasagna Pie

PREP 50 minutes BAKE 1 hour at 375°F STAND 15 minutes

WHAT YOU NEED

14 dried plain, whole wheat, or whole grain lasagna noodles
2   tablespoons olive oil
1½ cups finely chopped carrots (3 medium)
2   cups finely chopped zucchini (1 medium)
4   cloves garlic, minced
3   cups sliced fresh button mushrooms (8 ounces)
2   6-ounce packages fresh baby spinach
2   tablespoons snipped fresh basil
1   egg, lightly beaten
1   15-ounce container ricotta cheese
⅓   cup finely shredded Parmesan cheese
½   teaspoon salt
¼   teaspoon ground black pepper
1   26-ounce jar tomato-and-basil pasta sauce (2½ cups)
2   cups shredded Italian Fontina or mozzarella cheese (8 ounces)
    Halved cherry tomatoes (optional)
    Warmed tomato-and-basil pasta sauce

WHAT YOU DO

1. In a large saucepan cook noodles according to package directions; drain. Rinse with cold water; drain. Set aside.
2. Meanwhile, in a large skillet heat 1 tablespoon of the olive oil over medium-high heat. Add carrots, zucchini, and half the garlic. Cook and stir about 5 minutes or until crisp-tender. Transfer vegetables to a bowl. Add remaining oil to the same skillet and heat over medium-high heat. Add mushrooms and remaining garlic. Cook and stir about 5 minutes or until tender. Gradually add spinach. Cook and stir for 1 to 2 minutes or until spinach is wilted. Remove from skillet with a slotted spoon; stir in basil. Set aside.
3. In a small bowl stir together egg, ricotta cheese, Parmesan cheese, salt, and pepper. Set aside.
4. Preheat oven to 375°F. To assemble pie, spread ½ cup of pasta sauce in a 9×3-inch springform pan. Arrange 3 or 4 cooked noodles over sauce, trimming and overlapping as necessary to cover sauce with one layer. Top with half the spinach mixture. Spoon half ricotta cheese

mixture over spinach mixture. Top with another layer of noodles. Spread with 1 cup of the remaining pasta sauce. Top with all of the carrot mixture. Sprinkle with half the Fontina cheese. Top with another layer of noodles. Layer with remaining spinach mixture and remaining ricotta cheese mixture. Top with another layer of noodles and remaining pasta sauce. Gently press down pie with back of a spatula.
5. Place springform pan on a foil-lined baking sheet. Bake about 60 minutes or until heated through, topping with remaining Fontina cheese the last 15 minutes of baking. Cover and let stand on a wire rack for 15 minutes before serving. Cut around edges of pie and carefully remove sides of pan. To serve, cut lasagna into wedges. If desired, garnish with halved cherry tomatoes and additional snipped fresh basil. Serve with warmed tomato-and-basil pasta sauce. Makes 10 servings.

Chicken Caesar Lasagna

PREP 35 minutes BAKE 50 minutes at 325°F STAND 15 minutes

WHAT YOU NEED

9   dried whole wheat or regular lasagna noodles

CHICKEN CAESAR LASAGNA

2   10-ounce containers refrigerated light Alfredo sauce
3   tablespoons lemon juice
½   teaspoon cracked black pepper
3   cups chopped, cooked chicken breast
1   10-ounce package frozen chopped spinach, thawed and well drained
1   cup bottled roasted red peppers, drained and chopped
¾   cup shredded Italian blend cheese

WHAT YOU DO

1. Preheat oven to 325°F. Cook noodles according to package directions. Drain; rinse with cold water; drain again. Meanwhile, in a bowl combine Alfredo sauce, lemon juice, and black pepper. Stir in chicken, spinach, and red peppers.
2. Lightly coat a 13×9×2-inch baking dish or 3-quart rectangular casserole with nonstick cooking spray. Arrange 3 noodles in dish. Top with one-third chicken mixture. Repeat layers twice. Cover; bake for 45 to 55 minutes or until heated through. Uncover; sprinkle with cheese. Bake, uncovered, 5 minutes more or until cheese is melted. Let stand 15 minutes before serving. Makes 9 servings.

BUTTERNUT SQUASH
LASAGNA

Butternut Squash Lasagna

PREP 45 minutes ROAST 25 minutes
at 425°F BAKE 50 minutes at
375°F STAND 10 minutes

WHAT YOU NEED
- 3 pounds butternut squash, peeled, seeded, and cut into ¼- to ½-inch-thick slices
- 3 tablespoons olive oil
- ½ teaspoon salt
- ¼ cup butter
- 6 cloves garlic, minced
- ¼ cup all-purpose flour
- ½ teaspoon salt
- 4 cups milk
- 1 tablespoon snipped fresh rosemary
- 9 no-boil lasagna noodles
- 1⅓ cups finely shredded Parmesan cheese
- 1 cup whipping cream

WHAT YOU NEED
1. Preheat oven to 425°F. Lightly grease a 15×10×1-inch baking pan. Place squash in the prepared baking pan. Add oil and ½ teaspoon salt; toss gently to coat. Spread in an even layer. Roast, uncovered, for 25 to 30 minutes or until squash is tender, stirring once. Reduce oven temperature to 375°F.

2. Meanwhile, for sauce, heat butter in a large saucepan over medium heat. Add garlic; cook and stir for 1 minute. Stir in flour and ½ teaspoon salt. Gradually stir in milk. Cook and stir until thickened and bubbly. Stir in squash and rosemary.
3. Lightly grease a 13×9×2-inch baking dish or 3-quart rectangular casserole. Spread about 1 cup of the sauce in the prepared baking dish. Layer three noodles on sauce. Spread with one-third of the remaining sauce. Sprinkle with ⅓ cup of the Parmesan cheese. Repeat layers of noodles, sauce, and Parmesan cheese twice. Pour whipping cream evenly over layers in dish. Sprinkle with the remaining ⅓ cup Parmesan cheese.
4. Cover dish with foil. Bake for 40 minutes. Uncover and bake about 10 minutes more or until edges are bubbly and top is lightly browned. Let stand for 10 minutes before serving.
Makes 8 to 10 servings.

Rolled Lasagna Florentine

PREP 35 minutes
FREEZE up to 2 months
THAW overnight
BAKE 1 hour 15 minutes at 350°F

WHAT YOU NEED
- 1 egg, lightly beaten
- 1 15-ounce carton ricotta cheese
- ¼ teaspoon salt
- ¼ teaspoon ground black pepper
- 1 8-ounce package (2 cups) shredded Italian cheese blend
- 1 10-ounce package frozen chopped spinach, thawed and squeezed dry
- 12 dried lasagna noodles, cooked according to package directions
- 2 cups Tomato Base (see recipe, right)
- 1 cup Ground Beef Base (see recipe, right)
- 1½ teaspoons dried Italian seasoning, crushed
- ¼ teaspoon fennel seeds, crushed

WHAT YOU DO
1. In a medium bowl combine egg, ricotta cheese, salt, and pepper. Stir in 1 cup of the Italian cheese blend and the spinach. Spread mixture over cooked lasagna noodles. Starting from a narrow end, roll up each noodle.

2. For meat sauce, in a medium bowl combine Tomato Base, Ground Beef Base, Italian seasoning, and fennel seeds.
3. Spread ½ cup of the meat sauce in a 2-quart rectangular baking dish. Arrange lasagna rolls on the sauce in baking dish. Top with remaining meat sauce and sprinkle with remaining 1 cup Italian cheese blend.
4. Cover baking dish with plastic wrap. Place dish in a resealable freezer bag. Seal and freeze up to 2 months.
5. To serve, thaw in the refrigerator overnight. Preheat oven to 350°F. Remove plastic wrap; cover with greased or nonstick foil. Bake for 1¼ to 1½ hours or until heated through.
Makes 6 servings.
Tomato Base: In a large saucepan heat 2 tablespoons olive oil over medium heat. Add 5 cloves minced garlic and ¼ teaspoon crushed red pepper; cook and stir for 3 to 4 minutes or until garlic is golden. Carefully add two 28-ounce cans diced tomatoes (undrained), ½ cup dry red wine, ⅓ cup tomato paste, 2 teaspoons packed brown sugar, and 1 teaspoon salt. Bring to boiling; reduce heat. Simmer, uncovered, for 30 for 40 minutes or until slightly thickened and reduced by about one-third, stirring occasionally. Makes 5½ cups.*
Ground Beef Base: In a 5- to 6-quart Dutch oven cook 4 pounds ground beef, 1½ cups chopped onions, 1 cup chopped carrots, ½ cup chopped celery, and 4 cloves minced garlic over medium heat until meat is browned, using a wooden spoon to break up meat as it cooks. Drain off fat. Stir in 1 teaspoon salt and ½ teaspoon ground black pepper.*
*TIP: Freeze extra Tomato Base and Ground Beef base separately in tightly sealed containers up to 2 months. Thaw as needed and use in other dishes.

ROLLED LASAGNA
FLORENTINE

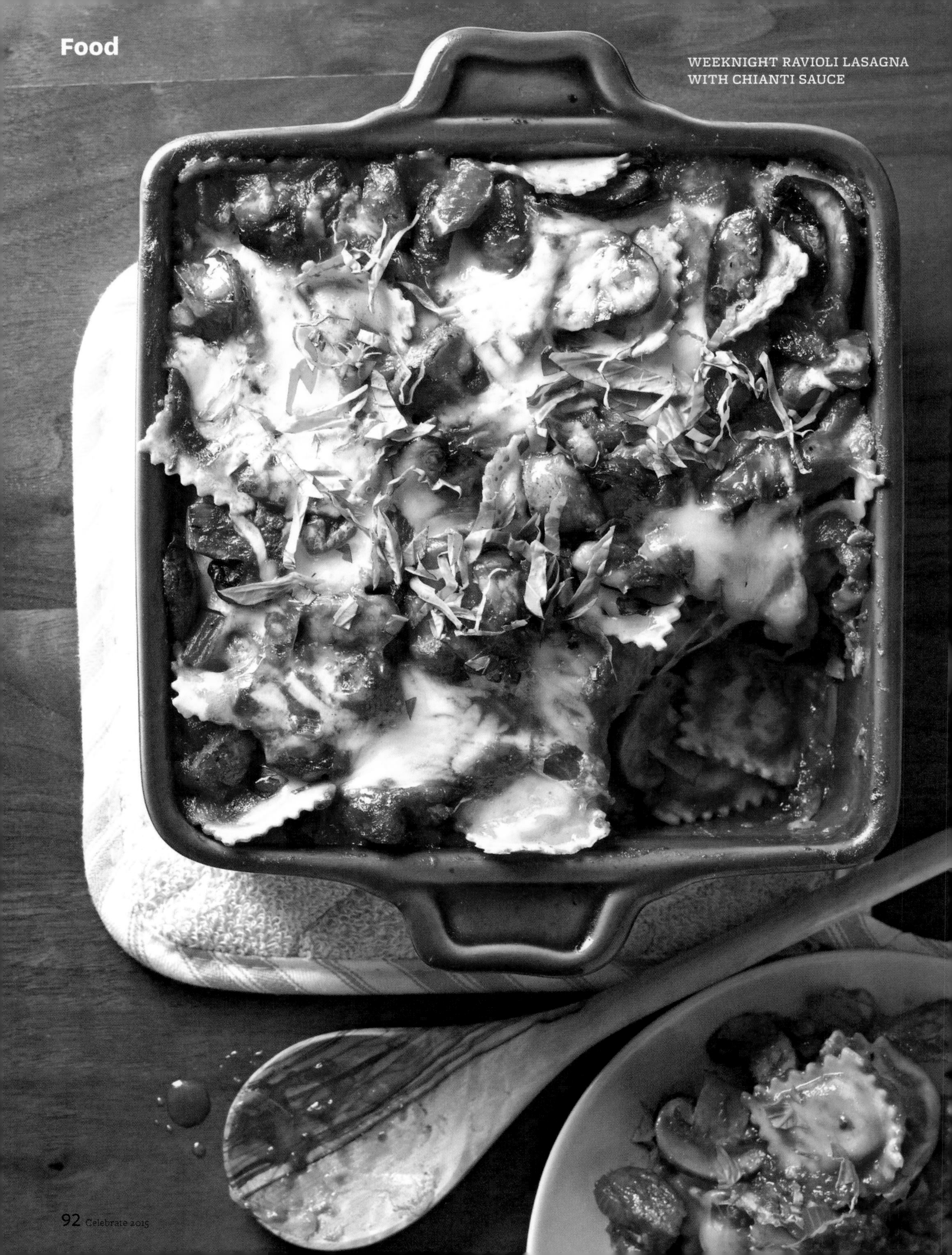

WEEKNIGHT RAVIOLI LASAGNA WITH CHIANTI SAUCE

Weeknight Ravioli Lasagna with Chianti Sauce

PREP 45 minutes
CHILL 4 to 12 hours
STAND 30 minutes + 10 minutes
BAKE 55 minutes at 375°F

WHAT YOU NEED
¼ cup olive oil
½ cup chopped onion (1 medium)
3 cloves garlic, minced
1 28-ounce can crushed tomatoes, undrained
1 cup Chianti or other full-bodied dry red wine
1 tablespoon dried oregano, crushed
1 teaspoon salt
¼ to ½ teaspoon crushed red pepper
1 12-ounce package cooked Italian-style poultry sausages, halved lengthwise and cut into ½-inch pieces
12 ounces fresh cremini mushrooms or button mushrooms, sliced
1 7-ounce jar roasted red peppers, drained and coarsely chopped
½ cup snipped fresh basil
2 9-ounce packages refrigerated cheese ravioli
1 8-ounce package shredded mozzarella cheese (2 cups)

WHAT YOU DO
1. For Chianti tomato sauce, in a large saucepan heat 1 teaspoon of the olive oil over medium heat. Add onion and garlic; cook about 3 minutes or until onion is tender. Add tomatoes, Chianti, oregano, salt, and crushed red pepper. Bring to boiling; reduce heat. Simmer, uncovered, about 10 minutes or until slightly reduced.
2. Meanwhile, in an extra-large skillet heat 1 tablespoon of the olive oil over medium heat. Add sausage pieces and mushrooms; cook until mushrooms are tender. Stir in roasted red peppers and basil; set aside.
3. Spoon one-fourth of the Chianti tomato sauce into a 3-quart rectangular baking dish. Arrange one package of the ravioli on top. Spoon half the sausage-mushroom mixture over. Spoon another one-fourth of the sauce over sausage-mushroom mixture in baking dish. Top with half the mozzarella cheese. Spoon

CHICKEN-ANDOUILLE LASAGNA

another one-fourth of the sauce over cheese. Repeat layers with the remaining ravioli, sausage-mushroom mixture, sauce, and cheese. (To serve today, omit Step 4. Continue as directed in Step 5, except bake, covered, for 35 minutes. Uncover and continue as directed.)
4. Cover baking dish tightly with foil. Chill at least 4 hours or up to 12 hours. Let stand at room temperature for 30 minutes before baking.
5. Preheat oven to 375°F. Bake, covered, for 50 minutes. Uncover. Bake about 5 minutes more or until cheese is bubbly and lasagna is heated through. Let stand for 10 minutes before serving. Makes 8 servings.

Chicken-Andouille Lasagna

PREP 45 minutes CHILL 2 to 24 hours (or freeze up to 1 month)
STAND 30 minutes + 15 minutes
BAKE 1 hour at 350°F

WHAT YOU NEED
16 dried lasagna noodles
1 pound cooked andouille sausage or smoked pork sausage links, quartered lengthwise and sliced
1 pound skinless, boneless chicken breast halves, cut into ¾-inch pieces
2 to 3 teaspoons Cajun seasoning
1 teaspoon dried sage, crushed
½ cup chopped onion (1 medium)
½ cup chopped celery (1 stalk)
½ cup chopped red and/or green sweet pepper
6 cloves garlic, minced
2 10-ounce containers refrigerated Alfredo pasta sauce
½ cup grated Parmesan cheese
 Nonstick cooking spray
1½ cups shredded mozzarella cheese (6 ounces)
 Grated Parmesan cheese (optional)
 Snipped fresh flat-leaf parsley (optional)

WHAT YOU DO
1. Cook lasagna noodles according to package directions; drain. Rinse with cold water; drain again.
2. In a large skillet combine sausage, chicken, Cajun seasoning, and sage. Cook about 8 minutes or until chicken is no longer pink, stirring frequently. Using a slotted spoon, remove chicken mixture, reserving drippings in skillet. Set chicken mixture aside. Add onion, celery, sweet pepper, and garlic to reserved drippings; cook until vegetables are tender, stirring occasionally. Return chicken mixture to skillet. Stir in half the Alfredo sauce and ½ cup Parmesan cheese.
3. To assemble lasagna, lightly coat a 3-quart rectangular baking dish with cooking spray. Place four noodles in the prepared baking dish, cutting as necessary to fit. Spread with one-third of the chicken mixture; sprinkle with one-third of the mozzarella cheese. Repeat layers twice. Top with the remaining four noodles. Carefully spread remaining Alfredo sauce over the top. Cover baking dish with foil. (To serve today, omit Step 4. Continue as directed in Step 5 for chilled lasagna.)
4. Chill for 2 to 24 hours. To serve, let stand at room temperature for 30 minutes. (Or freeze up to 1 month. To serve, thaw in the refrigerator overnight [lasagna may still be a bit icy].)
5. Preheat oven to 350°F. For chilled lasagna, bake, covered, about 1 hour or until heated through. (For partially thawed lasagna, bake, covered, for 1 hour. Bake, uncovered, for 10 to 15 minutes more or until heated through.) Let stand for 15 to 20 minutes before serving. If desired, top with additional Parmesan cheese and parsley. Makes 12 servings.

Easy Does It
Summer Sips

Sunset Sangria

In a large pitcher or bowl combine one 750-milliliter bottle chilled rosé wine; 1 cup pineapple juice, ½ cup vodka, ¼ cup triple sec, and ½ cup simple syrup. Refrigerate until chilled, about 1 hour. Stir in 1 orange, sliced; 1 lemon, sliced; 1 lime, sliced; and 1 6-ounce container fresh raspberries. Chill for 30 minutes. Serve over ice. Makes 8 servings.

Cucumber-White Sangria

In a large pitcher combine one 750-milliliter bottle chilled Sauvignon Blanc; half a sliced English cucumber; 1 cup green grapes, halved; ¼ cup fresh mint sprigs; and 1 small lime, sliced. Using a wooden spoon, press cucumber, lime, grapes, and mint against the side of the pitcher to crush slightly. Cover the wine mixture. Chill wine mixture and remaining cucumber half for 4 hours or overnight. When ready to serve, use a slotted spoon to remove solids from wine; discard solids. Add ice; 1 cup chilled white grape juice; remaining sliced cucumber half; 1 small sliced lime; 1 cup green grapes, halved; and ¼ cup mint sprigs. Add two 12-ounce bottles chilled seltzer water. Stir gently just until combined. Serve immediately. Makes 8 servings.

Strawberry-Basil Bellini

In a small saucepan combine ⅓ cup water and 3 tablespoons sugar. Cook and stir until sugar is dissolved and mixture just comes to boiling. Add ¼ cup snipped fresh basil. Remove from heat; cover and let stand for 15 minutes. Strain; discard basil. In a blender combine 2 cups sliced strawberries, the basil syrup, and 1 tablespoon lemon juice. Cover and blend until smooth. If desired, strain through a fine-mesh sieve. Chill for at least 1 hour. If desired, add ice cubes to champagne flutes. For each drink, pour about ⅓ cup of the strawberry-basil juice into a flute. Top with chilled Prosecco and garnish with a strawberry half. Makes 6 servings.

Sparkling Golden Sangria

In a large pitcher or glass jar combine 3 cups chilled white grape juice; ½ cup orange liqueur, such as Cointreau; ¼ cup sugar; and 3 tablespoons honey. Stir until sugar and honey are dissolved. Stir in 1 chopped nectarine; 1 quartered and thinly sliced orange; ¾ cup fresh or frozen sweet cherries, pitted and halved; ¾ cup golden or red raspberries; ½ cup fresh basil leaves; and ½ cup fresh mint leaves. Chill for 1 hour or up to 24 hours, stirring occasionally. Just before serving, add one 750-milliliter bottle chilled sparkling white wine to fruit mixture. Serve in glasses over ice. Makes 8 servings.

Watermelon Sweet Tea

Place 1 family-size tea bag and 4 sprigs of mint in a large pitcher. Add 7 cups boiling water. Steep 7 to 8 minutes or until water is a dark caramel color. Discard tea bag and mint. Stir in ⅓ cup sugar; cool. In a blender combine 4 cups seedless watermelon chunks, ¼ cup fresh lime juice, and 1 cup brewed tea. Cover and blend until smooth (divide into 2 batches, if necessary). Strain through a fine-mesh sieve into tea pitcher, pressing to extract liquid. Chill 2 hours. Serve over ice, garnished with lime, mint, or watermelon. Makes 8 servings.

summer

HAPPY DAYS

There's nothing like the good ol' summertime to put us in the best of moods. Flowers, sunshine, outdoor celebrations—make the most of it!

White Out

Flea market, dollar store, and crafts store finds get bright new futures with artistic layouts and coats of crisp white paint.

Blooming Coaster

One-of-a-kind coasters, found at flea markets, get a coordinating look when decorated similarly and painted crisp white. Choose coasters that have a wide edge. Use strong glue, such as CA, to attach several floral buttons arranged on one corner. Spray-paint the entire coaster with white primer; let dry. Spray with light coats of white paint until the buttons and coaster are all solid white, allowing to dry between coats.

Flower Fancy

A focal point for any room, this stunning cabinet offers a textural swag of everlasting flowers. The petal portions of the blooms are made from flea market tart pans (Photo A), candleholder cups (Photo B), and a bowl for the largest flower (Photo C). To make a project like this one, check flea markets and second-hand stores for rigid items in flower shapes. To attach to cabinet doors, drill a hole in the center of each trim piece while wearing protective eyewear and following safety precautions. Drill a hole in cabinet door where trim piece will be positioned. Attach each item in this manner: thread round-head bolts through the trim and door, then slip on a washer before securing inside the door with a nut. For flower centers, apply strong quick-dry adhesive (such as CA glue) to the opening of a wooden doll head and place it on the bolt head. Glue on wood buttons and leaf shapes to complete the design; let dry completely. Spray the entire piece with white primer; let dry. Spray with light coats of white paint and let dry. Repeat the process until the piece is completely white. For added durability, spray the piece with a clear topcoat and let dry.

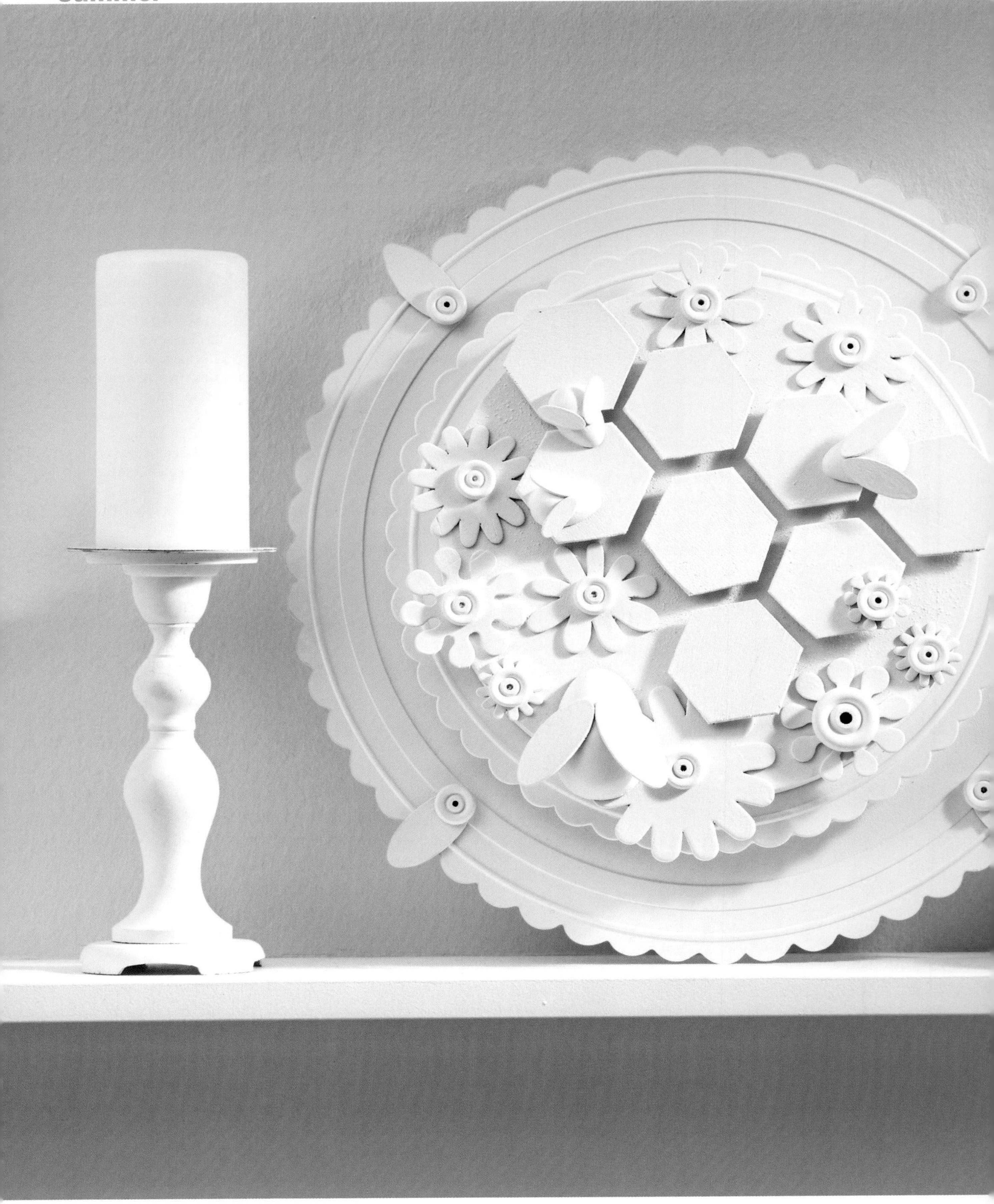

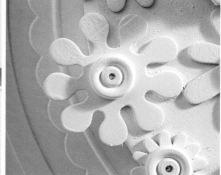

Busy Bees

Scalloped edged plastic plates, 16- and 12-inch, available where cake making supplies are sold, lay the foundation for this intricate bee-themed art piece. Because these riser plates typically have feet, find a small block of wood (or glue together several thin pieces) the same height as the feet. Glue it to the top center of the large plate to support the small plate. Glue the small plate atop the large one, placing glue on each foot and in the center to hold it to the wood block. Top the small plate with a 10-inch wooden circle, such as one cut for a clock face; glue in place. To make the design, trace the hexagon pattern on page 156; cut out. Place the pattern on $\frac{1}{8}$-inch balsa wood, trim around hexagon with heavy-duty sharp scissors. If the wood cracks, use a utility knife to cut the edges. Cut out eight hexagons. Sand the edges and top surfaces. Using the photo for placement, glue the hexagons to the circular background, placing a $\frac{1}{4}$-inch-thick wood spacer (any shape, just smaller than the hexagon) under each piece. Fill in the design as shown, using pre-cut wood flower motifs and wooden wheels for centers. To make bees, use half egg wooden shapes in varying sizes for bodies and oval wood shapes for wings; glue in place. Spray-paint the beehive design with white primer and let dry. Spray with a light coat of white paint; let dry. Repeat until piece is uniformly white.

Freestanding Cityscape

Your imagination will soar as you construct miniature buildings one by one. Use short lengths of lumber for the base of each building to give the arrangement enough depth to stand on its own. Use strong glue, such as CA, to adhere small wooden pieces to each building. Squares, rectangles, triangles, beads, golf tees, dowels, buttons, and more may be used to add architectural detail. Arrange buildings as desired and glue together. Let glue set. Spray-paint the cityscape with white primer and let dry. Spray with light coats of white paint, allowing to dry between coats.

All Aflutter

Nature inspires this captivating wall mirror. For this project, use a wooden frame mirror. Check out flea markets and second-hand stores or buy a new one. Cover the mirror with newspaper, covering the entire mirror and taping right up to the edge of the frame. Spray-paint the mirror frame with white primer; let dry. Spray mirror frame with white paint and let dry. Repeat if needed. Arrange a small bent bark-free branch on the right side of the mirror frame. On the frame, mark a pair of holes on each side of the branch near the top and again near the bottom of the branch. Remove branch and drill small holes where marked. Spray-paint the branch with primer; let dry then paint white. Also spray rigid dimensional butterflies available with garden décor or at dollar stores, with primer then white paint. Let dry. Use white crafts wire to attach the branch to the mirror frame, threading wire through drilled holes and securing on back side. Glue butterflies in place using strong glue, such as CA. Remove the tape and newspaper from the mirror.

Make Dad Glad

Crown Dad king for a day and give him
personalized gifts that suit his style.

Initially Yours

Dad will get all wrapped up in this cool combo. Embellish a flat frame with varying widths of wrapped twine on opposite corners. Then display a twine-wrapped papier-mâché letter inside the frame opening.

Cool Shade

Give a plain lampshade reason to shine using colorful bands of baker's twine. Wrap vertical bands around the shade, then add horizontal bands, weaving them under and over vertical bands. Hide twine knots inside base of shade.

Free 'n' Easy 4th

Celebrate the 4th with simple touches that honor the day.

Oomph Overhead

Create big impact with beach-ball size paper lanterns hanging in a cluster. If using over a dining table, hang high enough to allow table conversation without obstructing views.

Square Dance

Layer bandannas on the table for a simple runner. Using light blue and white keeps with the patriotic theme. Let red come into play with table or chairs, red foods, or centerpiece flowers.

Filling Station

Offer drinks, such as flavored teas, in big servers to quench thirsts throughout the day. Keep a variety of fruits nearby for adding extra zip to drinks.

Bandannas All Around

Dressed in holiday attire or not, everyone feels a little more special with a holiday hue around the neck. Guests may also want to tuck them in a shirt pocket, wear them as a headband, or tie them onto a purse handle. Remember to honor the four-legged friends at the party too.

Stack & Go

Dinner-ready trays are an easy alternative to setting a table. Drape each one with a bandanna or fabric square—in red, white, or blue—to act as a place mat.

Fun Zone

Kids love star-shape wands that add patriotic flair to bubbles. Tie ribbons or fabric strips to handle ends to make them easy to pick up and to dangle while in use.

Flashy Lanyards

Tie fabric strips to mini flashlights so kids can play in the yard before fireworks light up the sky.

A New Spin

Oversized for big fun, these patriotic pinwheels can be grouped as a decorating accent, used as party favors, or planted around the yard to catch July breezes. To make a large pinwheel, use a full square sheet of cardstock. For an even larger version, use spray glue to adhere two squares of wrapping paper back to back. Mark the center of the square paper by drawing an X across it using a yard stick laid corner to opposite corner. Use a drinking glass to draw a circle centered on the X. From each corner, cut along the line up to the circle. Bend every other point to the center, then secure tips to a dowel using a push pin.

Fair Fever

Step right up! Put a fair-theme spin on this summer's outdoor party and you're guaranteed to have a hit on your hands.

Set the Stage
Place food stations throughout the yard to add to the carnival atmosphere. Backdrop each one with paper banners and use stripes in limited colors to make it festive without being too overwhelming.

TICKET
KEEP THIS COUPON
TICKET
KEEP THIS COUPON
TICKET
KEEP THIS COUPON

Aww, Nuts

Nut cans get used a second time around holding peanuts in the shell. Just ask family and friends to save them for you so there are plenty on hand party day. The clean cans have a finished metal edge for a polished look. To trim, wrap cans with a strip of tickets, using double-sided tape to hold it in place. Finish with a ribbon bow.

Grandstand Garland

Showy yet super-simple, this garland adds midway magic. Choose two coordinating popcorn bags. Cut a notch in each bottom. Punch two holes at the top. Thread a length of ribbon through the holes.

Admit One

Invite guests to the party with ticket-style invitations. For the base, cut a 6½×7½-inch piece of red card stock. Fold in half to make a 6½×3¾-inch card; trim open ends with decorative-edge scissors. Glue a 3¼×6¼-inch piece of white cardstock to the front. Cut a 2⅛×3¼-inch piece from yellow checked paper and glue it 1 inch from left edge of white paper. Use the pattern on page 158 to cut the banner from light blue paper. With top edges aligned, glue to yellow checked paper piece. Top paper strip with a pair of tickets, available at party supply stores. Line the invitation with white to record party details. Delivering invitations in person? Replace the envelope with a paper popcorn bag.

Goodies on a Stick

On the menu, skewer some of the foods for extra fair fun. Fruit are a natural for spearing onto long skewers. To keep foods like cupcakes and cookies from sliding down the skewer, first thread on a candy fruit slice to hold the bigger treat in place.

Spell It Out

Large wood or papier-mâché letters in a classic carnival font spell out big fun. Trace around each letter on striped paper and cut out. To define letters, paint the edges black and let dry. Use glue stick to adhere cutouts to the front of letters. Shade paper edges with scrapbooking chalk.

Knock 'Em Over

Inspired by the popular knock-over-the-milk-bottle game, these party favors make everyone a winner! Find plastic or glass bottles at a party store then fill with small candies. Add a button-style scrapbook sticker to the front for extra punch.

Feather Your Nest

Don't let summer heat ruffle your feathers. Use these nature-inspired motifs to change up summer décor.

Fabulous Feathers

Spread your decorating wings with a pillow embellished with applique, embroidered wool, and felt feather motifs.

WHAT YOU NEED
1¼ yards white fabric
¼ yard tan fabric
felt, felted wool, or wool in gray, gold, light blue, rust, coral, dark teal, seafoam green, and cream
embroidery floss in coordinating colors
sewing thread
18-inch square pillow insert
FINISHED PILLOW: 18 inches square
Yardage and cutting instructions are based on 42 inches of usable fabric width. Measurements include ½-inch seam allowances. Sew right sides together unless otherwise stated.

WHAT YOU DO
1. Patterns are on page 154. To make templates of patterns, trace patterns onto white paper; cut out.
2. Cut the following pieces:
From white fabric, cut:
   1—17-inch square (pillow front)
   2—13×19-inch rectangles (back)
From tan fabric, cut:
   2—2×17-inch border strips
   2—2×19-inch border strips
From gray cut:
   1 each of pattern A, B, C, D, E, and F
From gold cut:
   1 each of pattern A and B
From light blue cut:
   1 of pattern A
From rust cut:
   1 of pattern B
From coral cut:
   1 of pattern C
From dark teal cut:
   1 each of pattern D and F
From seafoam green cut:
   1 of pattern E
From cream cut:
   1 of pattern F
3. Referring to Applique Placement Diagram, page 154, arrange shapes on right side of pillow front, spacing ⅜ inch from edges. When satisfied with arrangement, pin shapes to pillow front.
4. With pieces pinned in place, cut random notches in edges of each shape to resemble feather edges.

5. Use three strands of embroidery floss for all stitching. For stitch diagrams and instructions, see page 155. Using dark gray embroidery floss, stitch short running stitches along the inside edge of each shape (embroidery diagram, page 155). Using cream embroidery floss, backstitch striping details as desired on the gray shapes. Using light gray embroidery floss, backstitch a 2¼-inch quill for each feather. Feathers that extend along the left-hand edge and bottom of pillow front do not have quills. The feather at lower right corner of pillow front has a short quill that extends into the seam allowance.
6. Referring to Pillow Front Assembly Diagram, page 154, sew a tan 2×17-inch border strip to top and bottom edges of pillow front. Sew a tan 2×19-inch border strip to each side of pillow front. Press all seams toward borders.
7. Turn under ¼ inch on one long edge of each white 13×19-inch rectangle; press. Turn under on same long edges ¼ inch again; stitch in place to hem pillow back.
8. Referring to Pillow Back, page 154, overlap hemmed edges of back pieces by about 6 inches to make a 19-inch square. Edgestitch across overlaps.
9. Layer pillow top and back right sides together. Stitch around edges. Turn to right side; press. Insert pillow form through opening in pillow back.

Winged Welcome

Greet guests with a feather-embellished grapevine wreath. Construct each feather by wrapping and tying yarn onto florist's wire, then dip the yarn-covered wire into liquid starch and let it dry into a stiff feather shape.

WHAT YOU NEED

18-gauge green cloth-covered florist's wire
wire cutters
glue stick
acrylic yarn, such as taupe, gray, aqua, seafoam green, light tan, and dark tan
liquid starch
disposable rimmed plate
plastic wrap
⅛ yard tan linen
18-inch-diameter grapevine wreath
hot-glue gun and glue sticks
18-inch length of ribbon

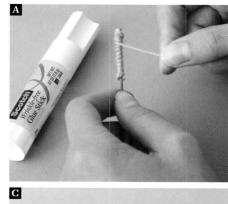

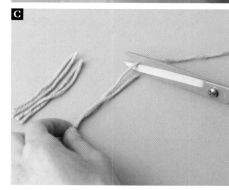

WHAT YOU DO

1. For each yarn feather, use a glue stick to apply glue to one end of a 9-inch length green cloth-covered florist's wire. Secure yarn approximately 1 inch from wire end on glued area. Wrap yarn tightly around the wire to cover the 1-inch end, as shown in Photo A.

2. When wire end is reached, wrap yarn to beginning, continue wrapping toward opposite end of wire as shown in Photo B. Apply glue to opposite end, wrap yarn over glue, then back about ½ inch from end. Glue end in place, and trim yarn end.

3. Cut 75 3-inch lengths of yarn, as shown in Photo C. Tie one length of yarn to the yarn-wrapped wire approximately 2 inches from one end.

4. Continue tying tightly spaced yarn lengths onto the wire to cover wire to the tip, as shown in Photo D. Leave the 2-inch end uncovered.

5. Pour liquid starch onto a disposable rimmed plate. Soak the yarn-wrapped wire in the liquid starch to wet thoroughly, as shown in Photo E.

6. Remove from liquid starch, squeeze out excess, and lay the soaked wrapped yarn on plastic wrap. Shape into a feather as shown in Photo F. Let the feather dry until very stiff.

7. Trim feather edges as desired, cutting a few yarn ties for a realistic look.

8. To make the accent flower, cut a 3×42-inch strip from linen. Cut 1¾ inch fringe, spaced ½-inch apart along one long edge of the linen. Roll one short end of the linen strip tightly; securing with hot glue as you roll.

9. Glue feathers and accent flower to wreath. Loop ribbon around top of wreath for a hanger.

NOTE: Use one color or multiple colors of yarn per feather.

Easy Does It
Terra-Cotta

Branch Beads

Add a pop of color among the trees. To make oversize beads, use two matching clay pots for each. For this trio, use three different sizes. For the mottled appearance, choose three coordinating colors, one for each set of pots. Load a 1-inch-wide paintbrush with the colors and paint Xs all over exterior surfaces of two matching pots to cover; let dry. Spray pots with exterior clear coat and let dry. Cut rope the desired length for hanging; knot one end. Thread a wooden bead larger than the pot drainage hole onto rope and slide it to the knot. Thread on one painted pot right side up. Thread on the second pot, upside down. Apply strong exterior adhesive to rim of one pot; glue the two rims together. Slide a second wooden bead on rope, slide to top of branch bead, then hang the art from a sturdy limb.

Standing Tall

Bring whimsy to the garden with everlasting blooms. Paint clay saucers contrasting colors, working from centers outward while blending in white; let dry. To make petals, roll out terra-cotta color oven-bake clay to ⅛-inch thickness. Use a mini heart cookie cutter to cut petal shapes. Roll three nickel-size balls for center; flatten. Bake clay pieces according to manufacturer's directions. Paint petals and flower centers, using method for saucers. Let dry. Use strong exterior adhesive to glue shapes together. Paint a dowel green and white; let dry. Spray all pieces with exterior clear coat; let dry. To attach flower to stem, glue a plastic vial to back of flower. Gently pound dowel in ground. Place vial over end of dowel.

Fancy Freehand

No need for a ruler. A 2-inch foam brush is the key to this checkered planter. Choose four or five acrylic paint colors plus white. Dip brush into one color and dab white on tip. Starting at top and working horizontally, paint a square approximately 2 inches wide. Dip brush in another color and white and repeat stroke, leaving a narrow space between squares. Paint squares in this manner to cover pot. Let dry. For outdoor durability, spray pot with an exterior clear coat.

Presentation Pots

Windmills, flags, or paper flowers—kids' craft projects make spectacular presentations nested in terra-cotta containers. Simply paint clay pots a color or two, and voila! You have a pretty base to poke in artwork. For a sensational base, plant greenery in the pots.

Beacon of Light

Fun for an outdoor party or to light a path, miniature lighthouses take just minutes to make. Choose two slightly different size clay pots to fit a lantern topper; paint pots white. Draw window-pane squares on each pot; paint black. Paint pot rims black; let dry. Dry-brush black rims with white; let dry. Arrange pots as shown, and the lantern, with candle, on top.

boo!

TREATS ALL AROUND

Wickedly fun, these creative Halloween party ideas and recipes will have you cackling with delight.

Crushing on Candy

Kids of all ages will love a happy-go-lucky Halloween party
built around stripes, polka dots, and piles of candy.

Point the Way

For a buffet table that beckons, coordinate patterned pumpkins with holiday treats and a banner made from patterned-paper treat bags.

Dressed for Excess

Tempt guests with a bountiful buffet with plenty of chocolate bars, candy corn, and other treats—all Halloween-ready with tags and packaging in traditional colors and patterns. Boost style with a candy-covered wreath and a stylish gum ball garland. To make the wreath, use low-temp glue to adhere candies to a plastic-foam wreath form. For garland, skewer gum balls with an awl, then thread onto string.

It's a Wrap

It's simple to upgrade plain chocolate bars with our wicked-cool wrappers, below right. Just print, trim, wrap, and secure printed paper with double-sided tape.

Grab-and-Go Popcorn Cones

For treats to eat while mingling, serve caramel corn in paper cones made from polka-dot bags or heavy-duty wrapping paper. Glued-on candies and ribbon add pizzazz.

Smile for the Camera

Clever candy-decorated pumpkins transforms a drink station into a fun-filled stop. Trim soda bottles with facial features cut from black adhesive vinyl, and decorate pumpkins with candy faces. Use low-temp glue to hold the features in place.

Crazy for Candied Apples

Dress up applies, October's favorite fruit, in party persona. Follow chocolate or caramel coating with drizzled melted candy, colorful sprinkles, or other add-ons.

Trendy Take-Home Treats

Send 'em home happy with paper pumpkins that are fiendishly easy to make. Just fill orange-and-white patterned paper bags with candy, and secure the tops with green Washi Tape.

Top This!

What's black and white and orange all over? A white cake stand adorned with black-and-white baking cups filled with candy—and colorful toppers. Even the pumpkin gets in on the polka-dot kick with a coat of white paint and black candies glued to the white surface.

Blue Magic

Step aside black and orange, rusted metal and rich blue set the tone for an upscale Halloween soiree.

Dinner Date

A little bit eerie and a whole lot of fun, cool colors, textures, and subtle holiday hints blanket the table with Halloween magic.

Classy Glass

A scrapbook sticker bumps glasses into party mode. Attach a small key to a wine glass stem using a fob or short length of chain.

Cast-Iron Clutch

Ornate cast-iron coat hooks hold rolled napkins at each place setting. If the metal is rough, cushion the back side with felt to avoid table scratches.

Shabby-Chic Candy Holder

What's Halloween without handfuls of candy? Carry on the sweets tradition grown-up style. Round glass candleholders with metal bases, reminiscent of crystal balls, are the size and style to hold a few delicious treats.

Well Worn

Search flea markets and second-hand stores for scratched metal serving pieces to blend in with table décor. Or use the same painting method for the plate charger, opposite. When dry, create scratches here and there using rough sand paper.

Eerie Etching and Charmed Charger

Place the date of All Hallows' Eve on each guest's plate for a sophisticated look that is super-inexpensive. Position large vinyl number stickers on the plate, as shown in Photo A. Brush etching cream in both directions over the center of the plate covering the numbers as shown in Photo B. Follow manufacturer's directions to etch the plate. Rinse the plate with water until all etching cream is gone; remove number stickers. To "age" a plain gold plate charger, crumple a paper towel and dip into dark bronze acrylic paint. Dab paint onto charger to create a mottled look.

Party Particulars

Announce your costume party with vintage-style invitations created with metal scrapbook embellishments and rustic papers. To make a card, cut a 4×5-inch piece of paper for top. Use sticker letters to spell out OPEN IF YOU DARE, as shown in photo. Use glue dots to attach a metal keyhole below lettering. Place key on fob and attach to paper using a metal brad. Mount to blue paper with glue stick; trim a narrow border. Mount to patterned Halloween paper; trim a 1-inch border. Mount to subtle-pattern black paper; trim a ½-inch border. Mount invitation front to a folded piece of white cardstock. Write party information inside.

Pumpkin Panache

Increase your chances of winning the neighborhood's most chic pumpkin award with inspiration from these totally cool designs.

Perfectly Packaged

This raven poses as a showgirl in feathery head-dress. Glittery leaves and sassy ribbons adorn plain or painted pumpkins for gorgeous gourds.

Lanterns

Light up the night! Cathedral-window cutouts, evenly spaced, give pumpkins lantern style for table, steps, window—wherever you want Halloween glow.

Black and white

Don't let these pumpkins fool you! The designs may look painted, but the patterns are actually created with tissue paper. Use orange pumpkins or paint with white exterior latex paint; let dry. Cut a 9½×12-inch piece of printed tissue paper the same color as the pumpkin. Secure tissue paper to pumpkin using exterior decoupage medium, piecing together as needed. Coat pumpkin with additional decoupage medium to seat paper edges.

Decorative Disguise

Coat foam pumpkins in black and white. Spray-paint some glossy or matte black. Cover others with book pages using decoupage medium. Top pumpkins with leaf shapes cut from book pages and silver paper. Cluster the pumpkins, raising up favorites in a pedestal dish.

Somber Ombré

Create this stylish setup by decorating pumpkins with black, white, and metallic spray paint. Add carved motifs after the paint dries.

Light Show

Pumpkins blaze in a brilliant bonfire—with no cinders, no ash, no alarming burn hole in your lawn. Cut flames, rather than faces, into the squash, then create a log surround. Stack the largest pumpkin on the bottom and smaller ones toward the top. Votive candles add the fire.

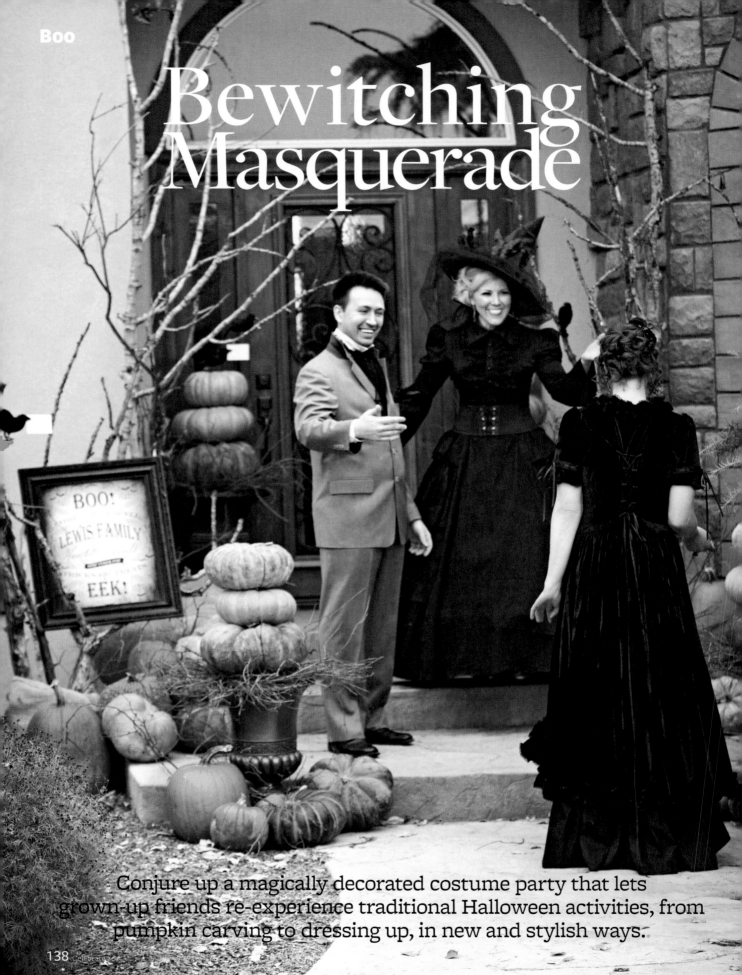

Bewitching Masquerade

Conjure up a magically decorated costume party that lets grown-up friends re-experience traditional Halloween activities, from pumpkin carving to dressing up, in new and stylish ways.

Illusion Initiation

Signal guests that they've really arrived with welcoming signage, piles of pumpkins, burlap-covered buckets holding skeletal branches, and eerie elements (such as ravens) that wondrously reappear inside.

Atmosphere Augmentation

Print "Eek!" onto cardstock and attach the panic-inducing signs to kid-size feathered wings wired to each chair back.

Enchanting Inspiration

Apply iron-on transfers to create temporary seat covers that remind guests to make their own kind of bewitching magic.

Scarifying Table Settings

Use free downloadable graphics (from labels to menus), handcrafted favor boxes, and funereally embellished setting to lure guests to the table.

Fiendish Photobooth

Even if you don't have an old-fashioned camera, you can set the stage for masquerade memories. Set up a spot to take photos of guests, arming them with Halloween props to grab when the mood strikes. Make a CD after the party to send to guests as a thank you for making the evening a spooktacular event.

Deadly Directional

Point posturing models in the right direction. Print "Smile for the Birdie" image as a face-forward sign to place in a skeletonized hand.

Cunning Characters

Bring the party to life by fashioning at least one life-of-the-party character. Dress a skeleton as a vamp with feathery head-dress, glamorous gown, and baubles galore.

Eerie Exhibition

Snap photos of skeletons wearing outlandishly grotesque costumes. Place the droll images in black frames then hang them with purchased skeleton cameos as a ghostly grouping.

Fright-Night Finale

Stage a tempting dessert buffet that summons ravens, witches, skeletons, and guests to gather for frightfully fun grub.

Pretty and Preserved

Cloches impress. Prop purchased skeleton-cameo cookies set on footed stands in glass domes. Abracadabra! Clear cloches become a fetching display.

If You Dare

Fun for favors, brew holders, or decorations, these bottles can be any size and set here, there, and everywhere. Spray-paint exterior of bottles black and let dry. Print and position a "poison" label on each one. To use as serving vessels, fill with small candies or a favorite brew along with a straw for sipping.

Spellbinding Cookies

Raise handmade or purchased Halloween cookies to artwork status by placing them on candleholders. Those with skewer-style centers make it easy for propping.

Devilish Delights

Stock candy shoppe shelves with labeled candy containers. Top the display with a "BOO!" garland. Print letters on white paper and trim into circles using decorative-edge scissors. Chalk edges with black and adhere to black doilies, flattened cupcake papers, or large ribbon rosettes folded from black construction paper.

Terrifying Toppers

Think beyond frosting swirls to magnify cupcake allure. Print out exclamatory cupcake toppers and set cakes in "Happy Halloween" wraps.

Enticing Tidbits

Make print-and-trim cardstock tags exceptionally noteworthy. Back them with glistening loops of black satin ribbon and rosettes folded from black printer paper or tissue paper.

Cut It Out

Employ butcher knives, meat cleavers, and cutting-edge signage to turn an all-American activity into a frightening spectacle. Encourage pumpkin carving in a friendly competition with free downloadable sign or make your own. Just print and cut out along the decorative edge.

In the Spirit

Conjure up a cauldron of sweet treats, wickedly wonderful pumpkins, and a host of bewitching decorations.

Whoo, Whoo Made the Punch

PREP: 5 minutes

WHAT YOU NEED

1   quart orange sherbet
1   12-ounce container frozen orange juice concentrate
1   liter bottle cold ginger ale
1   liter bottle seltzer
2   small navel oranges, sliced

WHAT YOU DO

1. Line a baking pan with foil. Place scoops of sherbet on baking pan and freeze until ready to serve.
2. To serve, combine orange juice concentrate, ginger ale, and seltzer in a punch bowl. Top with scoops of sherbet and orange slices. Makes 12 servings.

Layered Batwiches

PREP **10 minutes**

Kids and adults will nibble on bat sandwiches. Assemble the sandwiches with deli meat, cheese, and Catalina dressing, then use a cookie cutter to cut out bat shapes. Reserve the trimmings, cut into bite-size squares and skewer on toothpicks for guests who want just a nibble or two.

LAYERED BATWICHES

Ghoulishly Good Cookies

PREP **20 minutes**
MICROWAVE **1 minute**
CHILL **1 hour**
BAKE **10 minutes at 350°F for each batch**

WHAT YOU NEED

1 ounce unsweetened chocolate
¾ cup (1½ sticks) unsalted butter, softened
1¼ cups granulated sugar
1 large egg, at room temperature
2 teaspoon corn syrup
1 teaspoon vanilla
3¾ cups all-purpose flour
½ cup unsweetened cocoa powder
½ teaspoon salt

WHAT YOU DO

1. Place chocolate in small microwave-safe bowl. Microwave on medium 1 minute, stirring once halfway. Stir until smooth and melted. Cool for 5 minutes.
2. Meanwhile, combine butter and granulated sugar in mixing bowl; beat until light and fluffy, about 3 minutes. Add egg, corn syrup and vanilla; beat until well combined. Scrape down sides of bowl. With mixer on low, add flour, cocoa, and salt; beat until combined. Stir in chocolate; mix until well blended.
3. Divide dough into 2 disks. Wrap and refrigerate 1 hour or up to 2 days.
4. Heat oven to 350°F. Line baking sheet with parchment paper. Roll dough between 2 sheets of wax paper to ¼-inch thickness. Cut dough into 3-inch circles, using a cookie cutter. Place 1 inch apart on prepared baking sheets. Bake just until edges are lightly browned, about 10 to 12 minutes. Cool on baking sheet 2 minutes. Transfer cookies to wire rack to cool.
Royal Icing: Place 4 cups powdered sugar and 2 tablespoons meringue powder (powdered egg whites) in mixing bowl. Fit mixer with whisk; beat on low to combine. Beat in ¼ cup water; increase speed to high; beat until stiff peaks form, about 3 minutes. Add 2 tablespoons water and beat until light and fluffy.
To Decorate: Place 1 cup icing in a bowl; tint with black food coloring. Transfer to decorating bag fitted with #4 tip. Dilute remaining white icing with 1 teaspoon water at a time until the consistency of heavy cream. Decorate cookies as desired. Makes 32 cookies.

GHOULISHLY GOOD COOKIES

Make a Scene

Under a full moon, frightening flourishes and
devilishly delicious goodies transform a tabletop.
To make the moon, assemble a 20- or 22-inch paper
lantern and sponge white pearl craft paint over the
surface to slightly mottle and texture for lighting.
Let dry. To make the face, cut out shapes and apply
with decoupage medium or paint on with acrylic
paint; let dry. Place lantern light inside and hang
moon from monofilament. For pumpkins, use black
paint to brush on bold silhouettes.

DARE TO DIP

Dare to Dip

PREP **10 minutes**
MICROWAVE **3 minutes**

WHAT YOU NEED
1   12-ounce bag frozen shelled edamame (2¼ cups)
½   cup firmly packed parsley leaves
1   clove garlic
¼   cup tahini
¼   cup fresh lemon juice
1   teaspoon salt
½   teaspoon ground cumin
3   tablespoons extra-virgin olive oil
     Assorted cup-up vegetables and crackers for dipping

WHAT YOU DO
1. Place edamame in a microwave-safe bowl, cover and microwave on high for 3 minutes.
2. Transfer hot edamame to a food processor. Add parsley and garlic. Process until pureed. Add tahini, lemon juice, salt and cumin. Pulse until smooth. With motor running, drizzle in ⅓ cup water and the oil until well combined.
3. Serve with assorted cut-up vegetables and crackers. Makes 2½ cups.

Frightful Flatbreads

PREP **5 minutes**
BAKE **7 minutes at 425°F**

WHAT YOU NEED
6   naan flatbreads (4.4-ounce) or pocketless pitas
⅔   cup pesto
3   medium tomatoes, sliced
6   1-ounce pieces string cheese
9   large pitted black olives

WHAT YOU DO
1. Heat oven to 425°F. Place flatbreads on 2 baking sheets the spread with pesto. Divide tomato slices among flatbreads. Slice cheese into narrow strips; place in the shape of a spider web.
2. Bake flatbreads at 425°F for 7 to 9 minutes, until cheese is melted and flatbreads are crisp. Cut 3 olives in half lengthwise. Use for spider bodies. Cut one end of 6 olives for spider heads. Halve remaining olives lengthwise and cut into strips for spider legs. Assemble spiders on cheese webs. Makes 6 flatbreads.

FRIGHTFUL FLATBREADS

Creepy Caramel Popcorn Balls

PREP 5 minutes **COOK** 8 minutes **COOL** 4 minutes

WHAT YOU NEED
1   3.2-ounce bag microwave popcorn (about 6 cups popped corn)
½   cup (1 stick) butter
¾   cup firmly packed brown sugar
⅓   cup light corn syrup
1   cup M&Ms or candy-coated sunflower seeds

WHAT YOU DO
1. Microwave popcorn according to package directions. Line a rimmed baking pan with nonstick foil. Spread popcorn onto foil-lined pan.
2. Melt butter in a small saucepan over medium heat. Add sugar and corn syrup. Increase heat to high and bring to a boil, stirring constantly. Boil until sugar is dissolved, about 2 minutes. Cool for 4 minutes.
3. Pour sugar mixture over popcorn on baking pan. Coat a spatula with nonstick cooking spray. Push caramel corn into center of baking pan, folding over to combine. Coat your hands with nonstick cooking spray and sprinkle caramel corn with M&Ms. Using your hands, quickly combine ingredients and firmly pack into 2-inch balls. Cool completely. Wrap each ball in plastic wrap or cover until ready to serve. Makes 16 popcorn balls.

Grilled-Cheese Jack 'O Lanterns

PREP 10 minutes

WHAT YOU NEED
24 slices firm white bread
8 tablespoons soft butter
24 sharp cheddar slices

WHAT YOU DO
1. Cut out faces from 12 slices of bread. Spread butter on one side of each slice.
2. For each sandwich, heat a pan over medium heat. Place one uncut slice, butter side down, in pan. Top with 2 slices cheese. Place a slice with cutouts, butter side down, in pan. Cook until cheese is melted. Repeat with remaining ingredients. Makes 12 sandwiches.

GRILLED-CHEESE
JACK 'O LANTERNS

DEVILISH
CHOCOLATE
FROSTED
CUPCAKES

Devilish Chocolate Frosted Cupcakes

PREP 10 minutes
BAKE 22 minutes at 350°F

WHAT YOU NEED
½ cup boiling water
½ cup unsweetened cocoa powder
1¼ cups all-purpose flour
½ teaspoon baking soda
½ teaspoon baking powder
½ teaspoon salt
½ cup (1 stick) unsalted butter, softened
¾ cup sugar
2 large eggs
1 teaspoon vanilla
⅓ cup buttermilk
1 recipe Fluffy Frosting
   Sprinkles (optional)

WHAT YOU DO
1. Heat oven to 350°F. Line a cupcake pan with 12 cupcake liners. Blend water and cocoa in a small bowl; cool 5 minutes. In a medium bowl, combine flour, baking soda, baking powder, and salt.
2. In large mixing bowl, on high speed, beat butter and sugar until light and fluffy. Add eggs and vanilla; beat well. Reduce speed to low. Alternately beat in flour mixture and buttermilk just until blended. Add cocoa mixture; mix well. Divide batter among cupcake liners.
3. Bake for 22 minutes, until a toothpick inserted in center comes out clean. Cool completely in pan on a wire rack. Pipe on Fluffy Frosting and top with sprinkles, if desired. Makes 12 cupcakes.

Fluffy Frosting

PREP 5 minutes

WHAT YOU NEED
3 cups powdered sugar
1 cup butter, softened
1 tablespoon clear vanilla
4 tablespoons heavy cream
   Orange gel food coloring

WHAT YOU DO
1. Beat sugar and butter until fluffy. Add vanilla and cream. Beat until combined.
2. Transfer half the frosting to a pastry bag fitted with a large star tip. Tint remaining frosting with gel food coloring; transfer to separate decorating bag fitted with a large star tip. Pipe onto cupcakes. Makes 2½ cups.

Easy Does It
What a Treat

Boo Basket

Mummify a treat holder in a hurry with inexpensive gauze on a roll. Simply wrap a bucket, tin, can, or other round container, using hot glue to secure the ends. Add a pair of wiggly eyes to give the fellow a bit of personality.

Frightful Favors

For each candy container, glue black-and-white scrapbook paper around a slider box cover. Wrap ends of the box bottom inside and out. Cut out a felt frame from stiff black adhesive felt. Trace an oval (½ inch smaller than frame) onto yellow poster board; cut out. Adhere lettering to spell an expression (such as Boo, Eek, or R.I.P.) inside the traced oval, then draw a flourish. Make color copies if making multiple boxes. Cut out the oval. Remove backing from felt frame and adhere it to the box. Glue the oval to the felt frame. Add ribbon bows (or hanging loops for ornaments).

Can-Do Attitude

This elegant Halloween treat container is perfect for candy-hunting adults or as a mantel decoration to collect candies. Wrap a paint can or tin with a collage of seasonal scrapbook papers, adhering in place with glue. Line the top of the can with decorative tinsel trim, and shape a chenille stem for handle. Make a banner by printing a Halloween message on cardstock and trimming the edges. Glue a tissue paper circle to the center of the tin, add a glittery star, and top with the banner. Tie a snippet of tulle to the handle to finish.

Colorful Candy Bowl

Decorate a clear glass bowl for a Halloween-ready display. To make, cut construction paper into strips of various widths to use for stripes and trim. Trim with decorative-edge scissors if you like. Using circle punches, punch dots in various sizes and colors. Adhere pieces to candy bowl using double-stick tape.

In a Pinch

Make grand impressions using stickers to dress up jars, tins, paper rolls, and more. Printed or purchased stickers with orange and black trims quickly transform containers into favors fit for any monster.

Say It Like You Mean It

Make trick-or-treat candy storage a cinch! Print out free Halloween clip art (or design your own) on fabric transfer paper. Follow the manufacturer's directions to transfer design to the front of a cotton drawstring bag. Then head to the nearest house on October 31.

Patterns

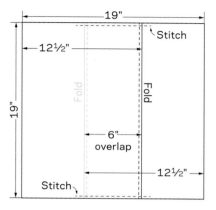

PILLOW BACK

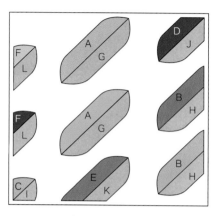

APPLIQUÉ PLACEMENT DIAGRAM

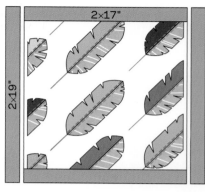

PILLOW FRONT ASSEMBLY DIAGRAM

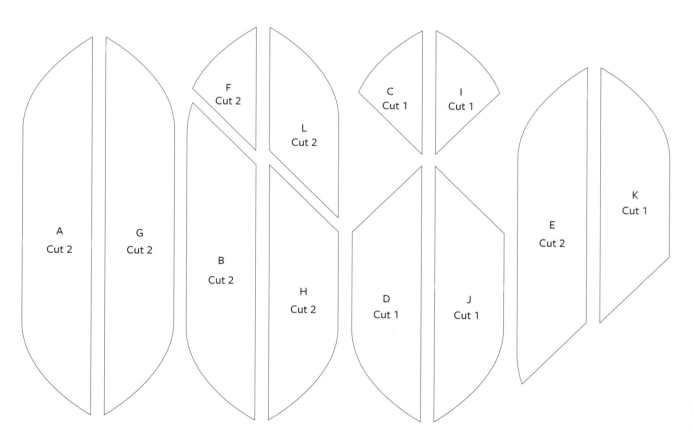

FEATHER YOUR NEST
page 118
Enlarge 200%

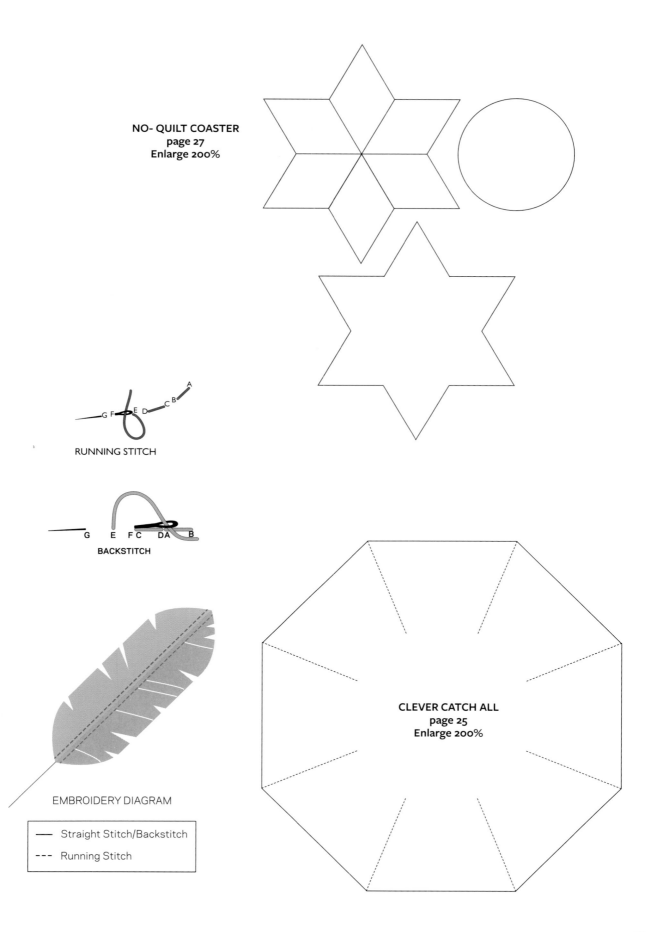

NO- QUILT COASTER
page 27
Enlarge 200%

RUNNING STITCH

BACKSTITCH

EMBROIDERY DIAGRAM

— Straight Stitch/Backstitch

--- Running Stitch

CLEVER CATCH ALL
page 25
Enlarge 200%

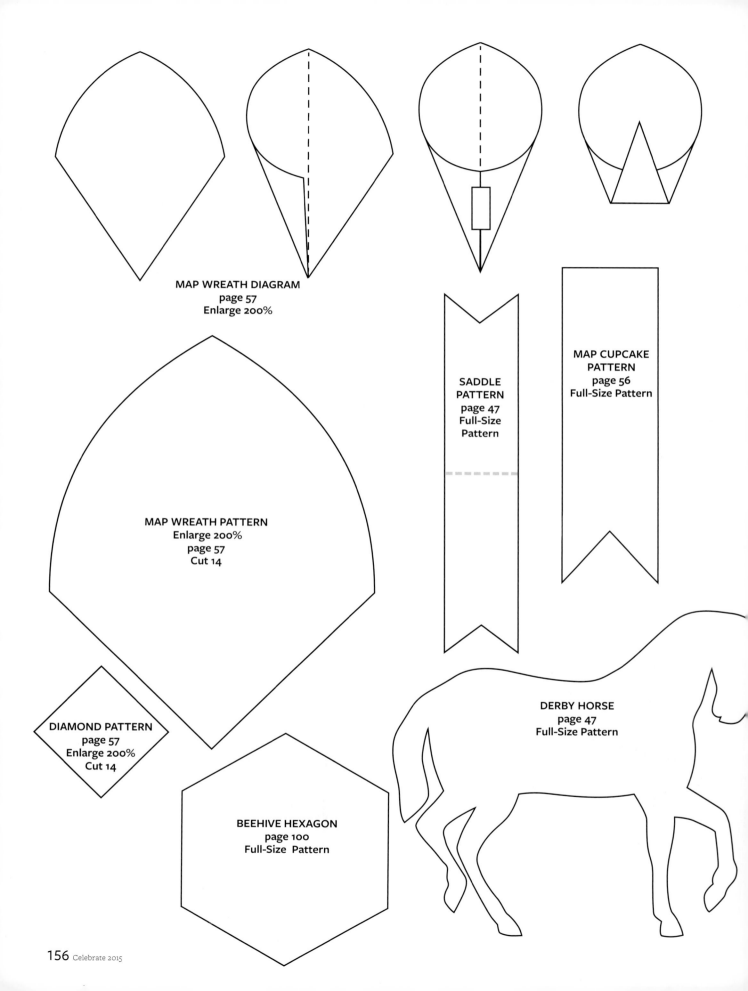

MAP WREATH DIAGRAM
page 57
Enlarge 200%

MAP WREATH PATTERN
Enlarge 200%
page 57
Cut 14

DIAMOND PATTERN
page 57
Enlarge 200%
Cut 14

BEEHIVE HEXAGON
page 100
Full-Size Pattern

SADDLE PATTERN
page 47
Full-Size Pattern

MAP CUPCAKE PATTERN
page 56
Full-Size Pattern

DERBY HORSE
page 47
Full-Size Pattern

DERBY FORTUNE COOKIES
page 47
Full-Size Pattern

DOODLES FOR MOM
TEA POT PATTERNS
page 53
Full-Size Patterns

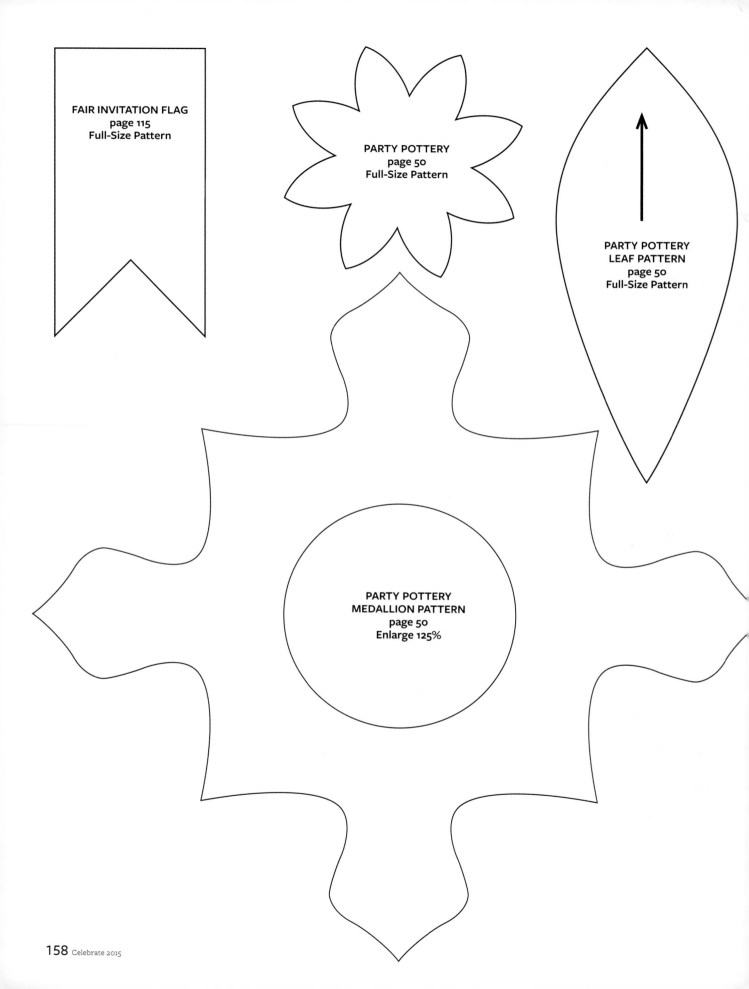

FAIR INVITATION FLAG
page 115
Full-Size Pattern

PARTY POTTERY
page 50
Full-Size Pattern

**PARTY POTTERY
LEAF PATTERN**
page 50
Full-Size Pattern

**PARTY POTTERY
MEDALLION PATTERN**
page 50
Enlarge 125%

Index

index *continued*

CREDITS

Photo Styling
Sue Banker
Cathy Brett

Photography
Jay Wilde
Marty Baldwin

SOURCES

**Paint-Your-Own
Pottery Locations**
paintyourownpottery.com

Special Thanks To

Glazed Expressions
8826 Swanson Blvd.
Clive, Iowa 50325